THE ART
OF
ACTIVATION

24 LAWS TO WIN, TO THRIVE, TO PROSPER, TO RISE

LUCINDA CROSS

The Art of Activation
24 Laws to Win, To Thrive, To Prosper, To Rise
Published by: Lucinda Cross-Activate Your Life Publishing

Cover Design: Hazel Lau
Editing: Robin Devonish Scott, The Self Publishing Maven and Kate Heister

Copyright © 2014 Activate Your Life Publishing. All Rights Reserved.

No part of this publication may be reproduced, stored in a retrieval system or transmitted in any form or by any means, electronic, mechanical, photocopying, recording or otherwise, without the written permission of the publisher.

Limits of Liability-Disclaimer
The author and publisher shall not be liable for your misuse of this material. The purpose of this book is to educate and entertain. The author and/or publisher do not guarantee that anyone following these techniques, suggestions, tips, ideas, or strategies will become successful. The author and/or publisher shall have neither liability nor responsibility to anyone with respect to any loss of damage caused, or alleged to be caused, directly or indirectly by the information contained in this book.

ISBN-13: 978-0-9905629-0-0
ISBN-10: 0990562905
LCCN: 2014911928

Printed in the United States of America
www.theartofactivation.com

Contents

Preface 3

Introduction 8

1. **Foreword by Dee Marshall-Switch Lanes** 15

    How Do You Spell Miracle? B.E.L.I.E.V.E 18

    Highways of Life ~ Maneuvering Life's Detours to Reach Your Destination 30

2. **Foreword by Nikki Woods- Develop Your Own Thing** 42

    Building a Social Empire by Embracing Your Inner Royalty 45

    Just Do You ~ Creating a Life of "Enough" 55

    Quiet Storm ~ Silence Can Be The Silent Killer 65

3. **Foreword by Vasavi Kumar- Action** 78

    Cut the C.R.A.P & Become Unstoppable 80

    Ring the Alarm ~ Arise Into Your Purpose 91

    Don't Stop 'Til You Get Enough ~ Recovering a Sense of Confidence and Authenticity.. 100

4. **Foreword by Tiffany "The Budgetnista" Aliche- LIVE RICHER™** 112

    Smooth Operator ~ Using the Power of Forgiveness 114

    Lovers Rock ~ The Journey to Self-Love 122

5. **Foreword by Nicole Roberts Jones- Find Your Fierce 134**

    Beauty and The Beast - From Depressed to
    Driven and The Seeds of Transformation 140

    Choosy Lover - Bad Girl Gone Graciously Good 148

    From Pieces to Peace - Recovering a Sense of Identity 159

6. **Foreword by Vikki Johnson- Women Are Powerful! 172**

    A Love Affair - Loving You is Easy
    Because You Are Beautiful 174

    Caged Bird - Going From Soldier to CEO 185

7. **Foreword by Gessie Thompson- Never Give Up 196**

    When Life Throws You a Curveball… Catch It! 199

    Earth, Wind, Fire - Surviving the Storm of Adversity 210

    Nothing Can Come Between Us -
    Building Family From the Heart 221

8. **Foreword by Nancy Matthews- The One 234**

    Kiss of Life - Live An Abundant Life Through Service 236

    Spiritual Electricity - Good Things
    Come to Those Who Pray 246

    Smoke and Mirrors - Keeping Your
    Vision Crystal Clear 253

Preface

The Art of Activation! There is a very good reason why this book is not called The Art of Distraction or The Art of Procrastination. It isn't in your nature to be distracted or constantly procrastinating. This book will show you how to unlock your greatest potential.

What you are about to read isn't a fad, phase or quick fix. The laws you will read are based on true life experiences with lessons that you can apply to your life today. I truly believe that Activate is a lifestyle worth living. What's even better is, you don't have to join a club, click a link, or pick up the phone for more information. All you need at this point is a pen, pad, your attention, and this book.

Don't worry, this is not homework and there is no test. There are no rules or deadlines. This is the beginning of a new chapter in your book of living an extraordinary life. I am almost ready to guarantee that not only will this book be one of the most rewarding books you have read to date, but you will enjoy it.

Think of these laws as pillars, like a support system for your life that will help you stand tall and inspire you to realize the kind of life you thought was only for your dreams. People with an activating attitude don't focus on what they don't have or what they can't do. They focus on what they have and what they can do. Don't spend your life procrastinating because you feel you don't have a better education or wish you were taller, smarter, or slimmer. Be grateful for what you do have and get on with living an activated lifestyle.

Based on my experience and observation, it's easy to maintain an activated mindset when things in life are going well. It's more challenging to stay activated when things aren't. That is when you have to push to stay positive and optimistic. Martin Luther King once said, "The ultimate measure of a man is not where he stands in moments of comfort and convenience, but where he stands at times of challenge and controversy."

How we activate when the odds are against us also determines our outcomes and results in life. You have to get to a place where you can activate the same way whether you are winning or losing. Giving energy to something is like feeding it. Mother Teresa wrote a poem that I think sums up The Art of Activation:

People are often unreasonable, illogical, and self-centered;
Forgive them anyway.

If you are kind, people may accuse you of
selfish, ulterior motives;
Be kind anyway.

If you are successful, you will win some
false friends and some true enemies;
Succeed anyway.

If you are honest and frank, people may cheat you;
Be honest and frank anyway.

What you spend years building,
someone could destroy overnight;
Build anyway.

Preface

If you find serenity and happiness, others may be jealous;
Be happy anyway.

The good you do today, people will often forget tomorrow;
Do good anyway.

If you give the world the best you have,
it may never be enough;
Give the world the best you've got anyway.

Activation is a daily gift that comes when we realize we have the power to make decisions. Just the thought of having control of what happens to you in life is liberating, yet at the same time, it is a frightening experience because with choice comes responsibility. The Art of Activation is about making your own choices and being accountable for them.
When in doubt, follow your truth. This way you don't make a decision that you will live to regret. Sometimes, you can be your own worst enemy when it comes to making choices. I read a fable a few years ago that put things into perspective.

A little girl was walking in the garden when she notices a small snake lying directly in front of her. As she reached down to touch the snake, it spoke to her. It said, "I am a snake. If you pick me up I will probably bite you, but I'm very cold and would like you to pick me up." The little girl ignored the snake's warning. She picked up the snake and held it until it got warm. The snake then bit her hard on the hand, and she started to scream and cry. "Why are you crying, little girl? You knew perfectly well what I was when you picked me up, and I warned you what I would do. I'm a snake. I can't help it. You should have known better than to trust me."

I share this to say that you have to be responsible for your decisions. This fable is valuable advice regarding The Art of Activation—knowing when to say yes and when to say no. A lot of wonderful things happen to me, and it's not because I'm more worthy than anyone else; it's because I've learned how to activate.

Activation starts with visualization. Many successful people, from business owners to celebrities to athletes, have used visualization to activate their goals. It's not a matter of when your dreams come to fruition; it's a matter of when. Michael Phelps, the U.S swimmer who won eight gold medals in the 2008 Olympics, credits visualization as one of his major keys to success. In his book *Beneath the Surface*, Michael Phelps says, "When I'm about to fall asleep, I would visualize to the point that I know exactly what I want to do: dive, glide, stroke, flip, reach the wall, hit the split time to the hundredth, then swim back again for as many times as I need to finish the race."

That's Activation.

It's easy to become discouraged and procrastinate when the path to our goals isn't a straight runway to success. Ask any successful person and they will tell you their character was built on their so called failures as well as their accomplishments. I often reflect on the unexpected turns my life has taken. I've had many successes and overcome my share of obstacles. I have been both financially stable and financially in the red. The trials, triumphs, obstacles, and challenges of my past have shaped me into a very different woman. I have learned to develop my strengths and encourage my weaknesses instead of using them as excuses.

Preface

What makes you blessed is the reason why you should wake up charged to activate an area in your life every day. I believe what makes me blessed is the ability to embrace change and be open to personal development. I wish someone had told me earlier about the Art of Activation and how it can simplify and amplify my life. My goal with this book is to show you how to live an activated lifestyle.

Lucinda Cross

Introduction

This book will change your life and will provide you with action steps to success, no matter what success looks like for you: success in business; attaining wealth, having loving and harmonious relationships; helping the less fortunate; or your personal health and wellness.

The Art of Activation© will give you key tactics and strategies to run in hot pursuit towards your personal, professional and global purpose. What these authors have discovered is that no success is possible without action. The Art of Activation© contributing authors talk about their challenges, trials and tragedies, as well as their victories and dedication of service to themselves and others.

In a world where self-doubt and pity run rampant, there lives a group of authors whose purpose is to enlighten you in the ways of self-love and success. They believe you can live a life beyond quiet desperation, waiting for success to find you. All you have to do is set aside your struggles, choose to embrace your gifts and talents, and decide to create a life that excites you. There are many ways to do this, but there are laws you must follow. This is The Art of Activation©, and these are the 24 Laws to Win, to Thrive, to Prosper, and to Rise.

As you read through the stories you will reignite your unlimited potential. Each law features stories, anecdotes and lessons drawn from experiences that are both informative and entertaining. The Art of Activation© your guide to realizing that power and living a happier and more fulfilled life starts today.

1. **Your Feelings Matter: Feelings unlock the fullness of life.** They turn what we know into an experience. They turn denial into acceptance, chaos into order, and confusions into clarity. Feelings can turn a meal into a feast, a house into a home, a stranger into a friend. Your feelings give you the strength and vitality to achieve your dreams and goals. Stop living in a state of fight, flight or freeze.

2. **Become a Servant Leader:** Pick up your sword of faith to win, to thrive, to prosper and to rise. It's beneficial for your success, and the success of others. Of course you can succeed on your own, depending on what success looks like to you. However, the support, encouragement, and love that you give and remain open to receive are absolutely vital to your success.

3. **Uphold Your Ideals:** The world offers every opportunity and distraction to erode your beliefs, values and morals. Don't give in and don't give up. The key is to not lose sight of your beliefs, values and morals. Trust they will guide you through any and every situation. Strive to live up to your beliefs, values, and morals. This is where your full potential can be reached.

4. **Listen to Your Heart:** Growth comes from the inside out. The heart never lies. Practice listening within. Listening will put you in tune with the things that are out of sync in your life. You will receive messages that will point the way. You will be guided

through every decision you make in life and it will bring you peace. All you have to do is recognize and act on them.

5. **Just Be Yourself:** As you embrace your authenticity don't focus on what you don't have and what you can't do. Focus and immerse yourself in what you do have and what you can do. Spending your life wishing and wondering if things would have been different if you had a better education, or that you were taller, smarter, better looking or born into a different family doesn't serve your future.

6. **For You, Nothing Is Impossible:** Never think for a moment your goals aren't attainable. You can achieve anything you set out to do. Many successful people, from entrepreneurs to athletes and celebrities, believe in the impossible and strive for it every day. It's not a matter of if you will achieve your goals; it's a matter of when.

7. **Embrace Your Knowledge:** When you embrace your knowledge you learn something new every day. Embracing your knowledge often means stepping back and looking at the situation and possibilities around you, rather than staying in situations that no longer serve you, making you unhappy, unhealthy, or both.

8. **Always Be Truthful:** They say "The truth shall set you free." This truth must come from within you and spread outwardly, toward others. To discover and live a fruitful lifestyle, we need to be honest. This might mean we need to change our vision, our conversation and or our environment.

9. **Attitude Adjustment:** Attitude is everything. If your thoughts are beautiful, your life is beautiful. The world we believe we

live in is in fact the world we live in. Adjusting your attitude will help you get through some very trying times. Negative thoughts result in negative energy. When you change your attitude you change your life.

10. **Never Blame Others:** You don't have to settle. Sometimes, you can be your best friend and your worst enemy when it comes to making quick decisions in difficult situations. Condemn no one, not even yourself. Don't wallow in self-defeating thoughts; instead focus on positive aspects of the life lesson. This makes you powerful.

11. **Learn to Manage Yourself:** The key to your success and happiness is personal change. Deal with positive and negative experiences wisely, and on your own. Through self- management you become unstoppable. By learning to manage yourself, you can weed out distractions that prevent you from achieving your goals.

12. **Humble Yourself:** What separates most successful people from the rest of the tribe is their ability to humble themselves by focusing on gratitude. Lack of humility inhibits us from reaching our goals and maximizing our potential. When we lack humility, we set ourselves up for failure. You gain more in life by being unpretentious.

13. **Don't Doubt Your Ability:** Your life is created by what you do. Small daily acts such as setting goals, smiling, and saying "thank you" becomes part of who you are. When you pursue life with confidence like an Eagle, you will develop a personal brand- the way you showcase your positive influence and convey the true essence of who you are.

14. **Create Clarity:** Detach yourself from any feelings of inadequacy and leave confusion and scarcity behind. Forgive and free yourself. Life gains clarity when we know and live by love and not by guilt. Clarity creates that personal mission that provides the foundation on which to build your future aspirations and internal guide for everyday successful living.

15. **You Are Obligated to Yourself:** You have an obligation to yourself to create an extraordinary life. Learning when to say "Yes" and when to say "No" is a powerful option. The path to live, thrive, prosper, and rise is about making your own choices and being accountable for them. Your "Yes", and your "No" comes with responsibility.

16. **Your Success Depends on You:** It's important to be realistic about how long it may take to succeed. You accomplish very little when you expect more from others. Instead, expect more from yourself. Your success depends on you. Many successful people will tell you their life was built by them moving forward even when the only person who showed up was them alone.

17. **Be the Change:** If you have been hurt, forgive and move on. People do what they do because of their own inner reality. It's not about you. It's about them, and their own inadequacies. To be successful you must not be the villain. Be the Change.

18. **Control Your Destiny:** No matter what situation you find yourself in, remember that you alone control your destiny by the power of choice. The world is made up of ordinary people who do extraordinary things every day. You must decide how

you choose to live. There can be a "Happy Ever After," or an "I Can't Believe I Shrunk My Life" saga. You decide how the story will begin and end.

19. **Reinvent Yourself:** Reinventing yourself is an important aspect of learning and growing. You'll gain the strength and confidence to inspire yourself to greater heights. Don't let your dreams and enthusiasm die because your goals present you with a challenge.

20. **Create Your Own Heaven on Earth:** It is important to have your own personal sanctuary. We all need a place to go and reflect, feel inspired, reconnect with our inner spirit and get away from life's distractions.

21. **Change Your Mind:** Make the transition from wanting something to believing that you already possess it. Whatever you want in life requires a mindset change. You have to believe you already have what you want or that you have what it takes to get it.

22. **Life Is Beautiful:** Your life can be what you want it to be. Keeping your thoughts, words, actions and values positive makes life easier to live. When you begin to live life aligned with positive change, you will understand exactly what your God given purpose is.

23. **Above All Else, Love:** Love will make you do things you've never done before, but always wanted to do. You can only make but so much money with your hands. How much love you can give and receive is unlimited.

24. Insert your own law here.

The goal with this book has been to show you how to live life without limits and boundaries. The laws are not meant to turn your life upside down or inside out, unless that is the reinvention you are seeking. Activation has to come from within. It's vital to develop a strong sense of who you are and what you desire to accomplish in this life. That's where The Art of Activation© comes in. These powerful stories, words of wisdom and laws are written to liberate you and prove that it's never too late to design a new beginning.

Switch Lanes

Because I understood that God created an assignment for my life, I had to move forward and step into all He created me to be. As a woman of great faith, the first thing I had to understand was that my business is a business, and not a hobby. It's more than a hobby when you have to make payroll. A wise friend once told me, "You're not in business until you can't make payroll." So I am in business. I had to release the defeating idea that the work I do is not just a passion but a piece of my overall purpose, a service to women who need it. As I moved forward with this new thought process I knew I would need help. Being a one-woman show would not work, and simply saying I need help would take me much further and allow me to produce much more.

Seeking motivation has been a natural progression for me. I would hear people speak and their words would catch my attention and resonate with me. Whether on television, via "Your Best Life with Oprah Winfrey," or in a book or magazine, I began to pay attention to those things that fueled me, and became more intentional about seeking motivation and creating a support system with those I had access to.

My Core Message of Activation

Be Willing to Switch Lanes! As a driver moves a car toward his/her destination on the highway, the car moves right to left and left to right. If you just go straight, the progression is slow and narrow. Moving from left to right and right to left is a progressive, forward motion that elevates the mind and self. What do I mean by that? Women must get off the road of average, status-quo, mediocre, and be willing to "switch lanes." One lane has God's plan and the other lane has God's promise, and going between the two will allow you to step into your authentic self and what He created you to be. Follow the light that God has for you, for there you will be happy and more fulfilled in life.

Activation Steps

1. Be willing to "Switch Lanes!"
2. Stay away from the average; it's not in your DNA.
3. Actively live and learn to master this thing called life. Be willing to share your story along the way.
4. Surround yourself with positive people, and run from those who nay-say and speak doubt. Keep your environment sterile, positive, and yummy.
5. Operate with blinders on. When focused on purpose, you can't see anything else.
6. Mind your money and keep money-earning possibilities on your mind that will give you the financial freedom you desire.
7. Invest in yourself both personally and professionally by constantly developing self. Instead of buying that new pocketbook, attend a seminar or conference. Become better and you will live higher!
8. Identify your resources of support and build a strong team.

9. Be the authentic you!
10. Be all that God created you to be.

Father God, in the name Jesus I ask that you bless right now. Bless whatever is to come out of this project. I ask that you bless the brainchild of this project. Bless her three children, her husband, and her enterprise. Father God, enlarge her territory. Use her gift to do whatever it is you have created her to do on this earth. Bless the project and bless my participation, my contribution, and Lord, let it be for your glory. Whatever you would have to come out of it, we believe you for your best. I ask that you bless every woman who will receive and who might dare to consume the content of this project. Lord we love and we honor you and praise you in Jesus' name. -Amen

__Dee Marshall__

How Do You Spell Miracle?
B.E.L.I.E.V.E!

Today, many are facing trials and tribulations of every kind, coming straight at them from every side. The economy is gradually trying to regain itself after years of unbelievable loss, the unemployment rate is still high, and families are in danger of separating due to an immeasurable amount of stress and pressure. The plain old life we used to know and enjoy has drastically changed. Looking at life today with all that we see and are experiencing, we constantly hear other people and honestly even ourselves saying, "It will take a miracle for this to work out!"

Well, truth be told, miracles are happening every day across this nation and around the world to people just like me and you who are faced with the same or even worse situations. What separates those who receive miracles from those who don't all lies in their power to BELIEVE! That's right—one word can change everything about your situation and turn it around for the better. Once you understand with certainty what the word "believe" means and allow nothing to change your concept of its meaning, then and only then will you begin to see miracles happening in your own life.

What is a **belief**?

The Merriam-Webster dictionary defines it as:
1: a feeling of being sure that someone or something exists or that something is true.

Therefore, our belief is something that WE PERSONALLY CHOOSE to form in our own minds about the way WE CHOOSE to perceive what's going on around us. It is our understanding that some idea or thing is true and valid and OUR PERCEPTION of life is based solely on our experiences and knowledge about life. Just because we see something a certain way does not necessarily mean that's the way it actually is in reality.

Perception is not reality and not until you know that can you really start to understand how to control your beliefs. Having control over your own beliefs is probably the most powerful thing you can do, and it leads to long-term joy and achieving miraculous things in your life.

Now we'll look at what it will take for you to **B.E.L.I.E.V.E.:**

*B*reaking the Spirit of Fear

Fear is a spirit that paralyzes many people and keeps us from achieving what we were destined to do. Multitudes of people never fulfill the call of God in their lives simply because every time they try to go forward, the devil uses fear to stop them. Is he using fear to stop you? Satan uses fear to keep people from enjoying life. Fear brings punishment, according to 1 John 4:18 (NIV), and you surely can't enjoy life and be punished at the same time.

Fear stops people in so many areas—spiritually; there is the fear of witnessing and using spiritual gifts. Emotionally, the fear of rejection has hindered people from beginning wonderful relationships, and socially, the fear of failure has held many back from beginning businesses and establishing successful enterprises.

God has not given us a spirit of fear, but unfortunately, many have received it. Fear will never allow you to unlock the power you have been given. Oftentimes, we receive fear from childhood before we become Christians because we didn't know God well enough to get rid of it. In fact, the Bible tells us in 1 John 4:18 (NIV) that "perfect love casts out fear." But where does this perfect love come from? One thing to be sure of is that it doesn't come from us. This perfect love comes from the Lord. God is love and the Spirit of God drives out the spirit of fear. The more divine love of God that we receive into our lives, the less opportunity there is for fear to get a grip in our lives.

I want to encourage you to take an inventory in the fear department. What are you afraid of? Are there any areas in your life that are being stifled because of fear? The enemy is always going to bring fear against us at various times. It's one of his major weapons—all of us must learn how not to fear the fear and step out in faith.

Daily make more room for God in your life. Make room for Him through much prayer, through more meditation on the Word, through verbally praising the Lord with your mouth, and with your music.

*E*mbracing Every Obstacle Optimistically

Life has thrown me its share of obstacles, and in the past, I allowed them to hinder my progress of moving forward with things I believed I was meant to do. Today, instead of allowing them to strike me out of the game, I see them all as opportunities to score a home run for the glory of God and the greater work of His kingdom. The obstacles that most likely first leap to mind are tangible, external things like time, family commitments, and money. But the obstacles that truly hold us back are the ones we place on ourselves; it's self-sabotage of the highest order. When these internal, self-imposed obstacles are cleared away, we become willing to break through any of the external things that hold us back and use them all as stepping stones to propel us higher, rising above what we are facing while understanding that our view of the obstacle is what will determine our success or failure.

If you're the person I used to be, the person that would allow anything and anyone to hinder your progress, I want you to know that today can be the last day you give your power away. Today is the day you can make the decision to "embrace every obstacle optimistically." *But how do I do that,* you ask? First, you have to see everything from the viewpoint of an optimist, meaning you'll now look at obstacles on the more favorable side and expect the most favorable outcome or lesson that can be learned from it and embrace it.

Many times, the very areas that we are challenged in are the areas God wants us to stay in. All of it is for a greater purpose which will only be achieved if we view our challenges knowing that something better awaits us on the other side. We live in a natural world but serve a supernatural God who allows absolutely no-thing (nothing) that we experience in this life to be wasted once surrendered to Him.

Loving Without Limits

Love—it's a word that we hear frequently today without truly understanding the depth and weight it carries. It's easy to say we love others especially when everything is going well and there's no pressure. However, what is your response when you've been hurt, rejected, abandoned or lied to? Do you still have the same love for the people that have caused you pain and hurt or does it now become anger and hatred? If you truly understand the definition of love, then you'll be able to move beyond anything that was done to you and truly love without limits.

According to 1 Corinthians 13:4-8 (NIV), "Love is patient, love is kind. It does not envy, it does not boast, it is not proud. It does not dishonor others, it is not self-seeking, it is not easily angered, and it keeps no record of wrongs. Love does not delight in evil but rejoices with the truth. It always protects, always trusts, always hopes, always perseveres. Love never fails." Wow, the Word of God states that love never fails, meaning it's unconditional without any limitations or conditions.

The love described in 1 Corinthians 13:4-8 on our own strength can't be attained. None of us can live up to this obligation, but the Lord has provided a way for us to do the impossible, and we know that with Christ all things are possible. It means you can love freely without having to place boundaries on loving others because of their actions. If we can just **love people for who they are, right where they are, just as they are** and let God their Creator work on all the other areas, then we have the love of Christ within us.

Loving without limits occurs only when you're able to fully trust and abide in Jesus. Surrendering and abiding are things you can do only through the power of the Holy Spirit. When we see a selfless Christian who can love like Jesus, we can be sure that person is abiding in Christ and Christ is abiding in him or her. What would be too hard on your own, you can do through this act of abiding. Continue to abide by reading the Bible, praying, and attending church with other believers. In this way your trust in God is built up.

Like branches on a vine, your life is a growth process. You mature more every day. As you abide in Jesus, you learn to know Him better and trust Him more. Cautiously, you reach out to others. You love them. The greater our trust in Christ, the greater our compassion will be.

When you live that truth, you can begin to love like Jesus.

Intensifying Your Faith

Faith is having a strong confidence or trust in someone or something. The Word tells us in Hebrews 11:6 (NIV), "And without faith it is impossible to please God, because anyone who comes to him must believe that he exists and that he rewards those who earnestly seek him." Let's take a closer look at what that verse is saying. Without having a strong confidence or trust in God, it is impossible to please God. If you believe God exists and know that He rewards those who earnestly seek Him and you're doing that, Praise God; you know your miracle is on its way. His Word says so and He's not a man that He should lie.

Faith, by nature, must be tested. That is the only way in which the things we believe can become part of us. It is the only way faith can increase. God cannot simply increase our faith by waving His hand. Faith doesn't work that way. But God will expose us to the elements necessary to test our faith, so that by working through them we might grow.

The way God tests faith is by exposing us to inconsistencies in what we believe. Think about how ironic that is. Our faith does not grow primarily by seeing only the truth. No, it grows by seeing and believing the truth and then by being bombarded by lies. It's the "resistance increases strength" principle. The more we stand by faith against the lies of the enemy, the more we grow in faith.

If our trust in God is going to grow, we have to learn to step out in faith, moving out of our comfort zone and taking chances. If we believe that God will sustain us for that day, we can be free to carry out His will, regardless of the consequences. Whenever we face temptations, fears, or doubt, God will always provide a way out so that we will not be overcome.

So keep a positive attitude about your own faith. Recognize that you have faith and that you can cause it to grow. Feed your faith and exercise it right where you are in your life.

Enduring to the End

The situation in which you need a miracle may seem almost impossible if you've been waiting any length of time, but I want to motivate and encourage you to endure through it and not give up. You have to determine that quitting is not an option and stand firm, holding on with expectation, and the assurance that according to Romans 8:28 (KJV) "all things work together for good to them that love God, to them who are called according to his purpose." The very moment you decide to give up could be the moment your miracle was about to manifest, and you cancelled its delivery.

We sometimes think that everyone else is happy except us, but there is no such thing as a trouble-free life. Trials come in all shapes and sizes and we all experience them. Wishing you had another person's life is a waste of your time. Thinking intently about what can be done to get out of your situation before it is over can sometimes lead to making the wrong decision or failure and ultimately having to repeat the entire process again because there was a lesson to be learned had you stayed the course. You have to endure knowing you'll overcome; don't try to escape it. There is also no escape from many of life's hard times. They must be endured. Rather than looking for an easy way out, endure knowing that a greater good is on the other side of it.

I remember the nightmare of an experience; it was when my husband and I purchased our home. In 2008, I sensed it was time for us to become homeowners and after praying about the situation, I believed God gave me the "yes" I needed to proceed. I was still growing in my walk and relationship with the Lord, but I was certain He said I could purchase a home. This started an almost two-year journey that nearly caused me my sanity, religion, and dear relationships with family and friends.

I would find a house only to be outbid by an investor. Because of the housing market crash, it was a buyer's market and boy, investors were buying up everything. Contract after contract was lost. The frustration was overwhelming, my energy level was drained, and my desire for a home was lost. By the time it looked like we found a realistic home, at this point, I was so exhausted I really didn't care much about any aspect of the house.

We submitted the contract, it was accepted, and for two weeks straight I drove past that house, realizing how much I hated the ugly-looking little thing. I prayed even more, asking God to get me out of that contract and promised Him that I wouldn't rush anything again or give up so easily and settle for less than the best He has for me. I have to say that God allowed me to learn a good lesson. The week before closing, my bank came back saying the house appraised for less than what the seller was asking. God made a way of escape for me because the seller wasn't willing to lower the sales price and as a result, the deal fell through. We continued the search and shortly thereafter, our realtor found us a larger home than the previous one, with more assets than we were hoping for and best of all, it was $10,000 cheaper than the one we lost. At closing, we walked away from the table with a check for over $2,000 which was our initial down payment because the sale price on this home was lower and because of the amount the seller contributed towards the closing costs.

After being blessed in such an amazing way by God, I've decided to endure all challenges presented until God gives me permission to move because I know on the other side of it there's a blessing I could never have imagined. I have endured and still am enduring in several areas of my life, but God has given me assurance with Galatians 6:9 (NIV), "Let us not become weary in doing good, for at the proper time we will reap a harvest if we do not give up."

Don't Give Up; You're Next In Line For Your Miracle!
*V*isualizing Your Victory

Quit analyzing your problems and start visualizing your victory. It's time to retire from dreaming the dream to living God's dream for your life. Something beautiful happens when you can see yourself on the other side of the finish line despite what life throws your way. Vision is what we see, but it is also the way in which we see. Vision is the lens that interprets the events of our life, the way we view people and our concept of God. If we have a scratch on our glasses, it may seem like everybody around us has scratches too, but the problem actually lies with us because our vision is impaired. Jesus said that our eyes are the windows of our hearts. In other words, we perceive with our eyes but we see with our hearts. Our minds receive images from our eyes but our hearts interpret these images. If our hearts become bitter, jealous, hurt, or in some way infected, the lens of our hearts are distorted. What we perceive is happening and what is really going on could be two completely different things.

Proverbs 29:18 (KJV) says, "Where there is no vision, the people perish: but he that keepeth the law, happy is he." This proverb clearly tells us that we perish without vision. If you don't have a visual of where you're going, how do you know if you're headed in the right direction? Vision is the bridge between the present and the future. Habakkuk 2:2-3 (KJV) says, "And the Lord answered me, and said, 'Write the vision, and make it plain upon tables, that he may run that readeth it. For the vision is yet for an appointed time, but at the end it shall speak, and not lie: though it tarry, wait for it; because it will surely come, it will not tarry.'" We are told to write it down; God has promised us victory and the first part of accomplishing any vision is to take it from the unseen world and bring it into the natural realm. This can be accomplished by simply writing down the vision. Expressing the vision on paper pulls the dream that is in your spirit (that no one can see but you) into the visible world.

Expectancy (EXPECT & SEE)

In life, we're always waiting for something—for a dream to come to pass, to meet the right person, for a problem to turn around—much of life is spent waiting. However, there's a right way to wait and a wrong way to wait, and according to Isaiah 40:31 (NIV), "Those who hope (wait) in the Lord will renew their strength. They will soar on wings like eagles; they will run and not grow weary, they will walk and not be faint."

When we hear that word "wait," most people think that means do nothing and be passive, which actually is incorrect. I would argue that the word "wait" really means that "you're moving with direction and preparing for what you expect, hope, and seek." You prayed, you believed, and now you're looking for God's goodness; you're expecting your health to improve, you're expecting new doors to open, you're expecting to have a blessed year… that's what it really means to wait.

When you're waiting expectantly, you know today could be the day you get the break you need or the day your problem turns around. There's anticipation in your spirit, you talk and act like it's going to happen, and you're on the lookout for it.

Now is the time to ACTIVATE and allow every door of opportunity to be opened for the miracle to manifest in your life. It's time to move beyond where you are today, welcoming others alongside who will stretch you beyond your comfort zone while motivating you to press beyond the difficulties as they arise.

Make the decision to love unconditionally, forgiving all who have wronged you, while allowing your faith to be strengthened as your dreams and visions become a reality simply because you made the decision to BELIEVE and took the steps required for them to be achieved.

Continue to trust in the promises, EXPECT AND SEE the manifestation, and BELIEVE.

Monique Strachan-Murray

Highways of Life
Maneuvering Life's Detours to Reach Your Destination

For those of us who are accustomed to taking road trips, detours are our least favorite things to experience. If you've ever taken a road trip, you are familiar with these detours that take us off course: road blocks, accidents, construction, unexpected weather, as well as fatigue, weariness, and sleepy drivers that can put us in harm's way. Some of these detours are so discouraging, they give us the urge to turn around and go back home, but we don't because either we've traveled too far to turn around or we're determined to reach our planned destination—especially if it's a trip we've been planning for a very long time. Somehow, the detours seem to be worth the effort.

Much like road trips, we experience detours in our lives as well. When life's detours show up, we must have the same tenacity to continue. We can handle them the same way we handle the detours on a road trip; we just have to remember that our commitment to life is both worth the journey and the destination. The detours in our lives are transformations we go through in order to reach the place of maturity designed to help us reach our destinations.

Many of us have goals we've set for our lives and have mapped out the routes required for getting us there without considering the detours. This is most certainly the story of my life. My detours have been many, but my maneuvering tactics have also been plenty. W.E.B. Du Bois said it best: *"There is no force equal to a woman determined to rise."* I was certainly determined to rise and arrive.

My detours may seem a little minute to some, but to me they were detours I most certainly had to get around in order to make it to where I was destined to go. I found I was constantly comparing myself to others around me. Not with those whose situations were more challenging than mine, but with those who I saw as achieving the success I wanted to achieve. My thought process was, "I wish I was able to have a nice professional job like my friend Jill," or "Why am I still going to college when all my friends have graduated?" Comparison was something I struggled with for a long time and every now and then I still need to do a reality check-in with myself.

This comparison worsened when I became pregnant while attending college. I thought my world was going to crumble as society had predicted. Because I grew up in an African American, single-parent household, statistics said I would end up the same way or even worse. There I was on a path that had already been predestined for me, or so I thought. I dropped out of college and got a temporary job working as an administrative assistant, making a little more than minimum wage while preparing to become a mother. I had never really given much thought to becoming a mother until that point. I must say, my heart was forever changed when I held my baby girl in my arms for the first time.

It was at that moment the life I was living was not the life I wanted for myself and surely not for my daughter. Sophia Loren said it so eloquently: *"When you are a mother, you are really never alone in your thoughts. A mother always has to think twice, once for herself and once for her child."* I was determined to no longer turn around and go back when I stumbled upon a detour; I was determined to go through them to get to the other side for myself and my family. Despite the excuses I had to eliminate from my mindset such as not having enough money, not having enough time, and having to juggle affordable childcare and my work schedule, I enrolled in college again to complete my undergraduate degree. I was not going to succumb to the detours I experienced and let the life-changing opportunity of graduating college get away from me.

Thomas Friedman stated, *"Big breakthroughs happen when what is suddenly possible meets what is desperately necessary."* I was looking at the fact that it could possibly take me ten years to get my bachelor's degree because of the lost time and a fair amount of lost credits in the transfer process. However, during this time, I created much of my own anxiety by looking at where everyone else was and not where I was and where I was going. I was so distracted by others' successes, I didn't see my own. I couldn't enjoy my own accomplishments. My sister and most of my friends were finishing their graduate degrees and here I was, still on my "tricycle" trying to get my first bachelor's degree.

I didn't acknowledge that I was working a full-time job, going to college full-time, and was enlisted in the Army Reserve, all while being a mom to an inquisitive, fast-growing two-year-old. Not to mention the fact that I was maintaining a 3.0 GPA and made the Dean's List. I was achieving success where I was but was too blind to see it. It was not jealousy or envy; I was genuinely happy for my friends and their successes, but I just couldn't come out of the state of comparison and wishing I was further along than I was. I finally came to the realization that

God had given me the talents and skills to move to my next level and it was my responsibility to use what He gave me, for my own good as well as my daughter's and those whose lives I would later impact. I was on a detour, but I was determined to find my way back to the main highway.

I had to realize that we all have different life experiences, perceptions, and baggage. Most often, we all have the same information we need to handle heavy baggage, but sometimes fear takes control. Fear is powerful and can sometimes be paralyzing to those who are unable to see it as a temporary route; they can find their way back. That fear could be keeping you from going back to school. It's a detour and it's telling you that "you are not smart enough, you can't afford it, and you barely have time to get things done now." It's telling you that "you aren't ready, and you don't know enough." Fear is even telling you that someone else can do a better job, especially when you're up for a promotion at work. You have to ask yourself: *how am I managing the situation? How am I going to get back on the right road after being detoured? How am I looking at the consequences of my decision? Do I believe I can be successful and receive my increase and favor or have I succumbed to my situation and surrendered to my fears?*

At this point, it's time to come to the realization that the detour is temporary. Preparation is crucial to achieving your next level and getting you back on the right track. The greatest moment of transforming your life, heart, mind, and soul lies ahead and it's going to be life-altering and miraculous. You will become a new creation, ready for the next chapter. You will also fully appreciate your present situation and seek excellence where you are. The first thing you should do is NOT compare yourself to your neighbors, family members, or friends. We do not all start in the same place; therefore, we won't all finish at the same time.

You have to remember that transforming is not easy. When I think of transformational living and the various life stages, I think of one of the most miraculous transformations of nature: the butterfly. Just when the caterpillar thinks life is over, it becomes a butterfly. A caterpillar achieves this transformation through a series of changes in different stages of its life. This metamorphosis is similar to what we can experience as we go through various stages and changes in life. Whether it's a new job, the birth of a child, going back to school, divorce, or any other life-altering situation, we are all guaranteed to experience at least one of these, and most likely several.

To think a tiny, furry worm can turn into a beautiful butterfly… this is an indication of what can happen over time. For the caterpillar, death is the pathway to becoming a new, adult butterfly. It begins to digest its own tissues; some disappear and some are recycled and become liquefied as the new life is formed. What a wonderful analogy of what life can and will be after our own transformational experiences! Finding your way back to the main highway after being detoured is a wonderful feeling because the detour most likely took you through unfamiliar places.

This is when the storm may seem the greatest, when you want to give up, when hope is fading and despair is becoming your best friend. But know that this storm is just before the sunrise. You have within you techniques that will help you maneuver through life's detours and place you on the right track to your destination. This is the place where you might lose friends and possibly even loved ones. You will have to adopt a new way of thinking, find new avenues to travel. Doing the same thing over and over again will yield the same result, but trying something new just may produce different results. Don't think that this phase will come without struggles or sacrifices. If it didn't include these, the changes wouldn't be worth it.

When I started attending college again, I sacrificed sleep and used vacation time to study for exams and to prepare projects. I had to see how these choices affected the outcomes I wanted. Being able to provide for my daughter was worth it. Being able to walk across that stage for my diploma was worth it. Being able to get back on the right track was well worth it. By all accounts, these choices were improving my life, my daughter's life, and others' lives in the future. Over the years, I have used the same tenacity to earn two graduate degrees and achieve the success I aspired.

If you look closely at a cocoon just before the butterfly is ready to emerge, you will begin to see the exquisite colors of the butterfly beginning to form. As you are going through your struggles and transformation is taking place, the people around you will begin to see small flickers of who you are becoming and you'll begin to set the expectations of those around you. It is then that the wings emerge. For you, this is where you will see how all your planning and foresight has come to fruition. It is when you will see what you created. You will experience results from the transformation in your heart, your mind, and your soul.

Although we may go through similar challenges, transformation can look a little different for everyone; you may go through them quickly or at a slower rate. These transformations build you up so you can take on new things as opportunities present themselves. They will help you to become unstuck, to stay motivated, and to keep your eyes on the prize. Within seven years after completing my bachelor's degree, I was able to complete my MBA and doctorate degrees and took on one of my most challenging positions to date: a senior position with a major brand company. This was not somewhere I would have imagined myself ten years earlier. However, having gone through previous challenges and transformations, I knew that with perseverance, hard work, time, financial investments in myself, and the support of great mentors along the way, I had a chance at being successful in my new role. I was not willing to let fear drive my direction anymore. I had gained a greater confidence in my abilities and had the skill set that would be transferable to take advantage of this opportunity. As I became more familiar with the requirements of the job, the only question I asked myself was, "Why *not* me?"

We all have or know someone who has had life's circumstances detour them yet they were able to get back on the right track—sometimes to our amazement and wonder. We all have the ability to find our way back and should never feel the need to surrender or turn around and go back. When life's detours take you by surprise, you need to look at your situation and strategize a plan to reroute you back on track. It will be important to know where you are to figure out where you are going. This will allow you to put a plan in place systematically from a holistic perspective. Since everything is interconnected in what we do, it is important to keep this perspective in mind when planning and making decisions, all while keeping yourself as the main stakeholder. Oftentimes we get too distracted by the interconnectedness of the web and we make decisions based on others rather than ourselves.

Remember, it goes back to sacrifice. You have to be willing to struggle and sacrifice through the process to achieve true transformation that is life-changing. A promotion may require more hours in the office, which means less time at home with family. Perhaps the answer is using some of your extra income to hire a cleaning person to free up your Saturday mornings to spend with the family, or have someone prepare a couple of meals in advance so you can still have dinner with the family the days you work a little later. This may allow you to accept the new position you have been dreaming about rather than seeing it as a struggle or sacrifice to the family. It's about being able to look at that caterpillar and admire it for what it is capable of doing and becoming. Know that everything and everyone, especially you, has worth. With a little faith, you can now believe in yourself, plant a seed, and rise up to your next level, receiving your increase.

So, what do you want in your next chapter? Are you who you want to be, where you want to be, and doing what you want to do? Have your achievements been meaningful? Have you had to sacrifice things that you value? Have you run into a detour that has you wanting to turn back? The charge is to help you find balance for all the things that are important to you while still taking care of yourself and the people who are important to you. A "life map" was the tool I used to help me make it through the detours. I used it to achieve my goals and to start living the life I imagined. I saw it as my personal PIP (Performance Improvement Plan), similar to what is used in the workplace. I identified the areas in my personal and professional life that I wanted to improve to create the transformations I wanted. Creating an effective life map serves as an action plan for your personal and/or professional goals. A life map will guide you from where you are to where you want to go, and put your goals in focus. It is important in this process that you do not focus on the past, but take a holistic approach. See yourself at your destination before you even get there. Take into consideration all facets of your being, your mind, body, and spirit. You'll discover what works best for you so you can set goals and make real and sustainable choices that support you in living a healthy and well-balanced life. It puts you in charge of your own life and secures the future you have been envisioning.

During my doctoral studies, I was introduced to Peter Senge and the concept of "systems thinking." Systems thinking is the process of understanding how things influence each other within a whole, which can help us understand and change complicated systems such as life. Senge discusses three characteristics of a systems thinking approach:

1. This must involve a very deep and persistent commitment to "real learning."

2. Be prepared to be wrong. Our way of seeing things is often part of the problem.

3. You need to get people with different points of views who are seeing different parts of the system come together collectively.

Using this thinking in the creation of your life map makes it "action-oriented" and applied from a "systematic" framework to enhance your life goals. For the purpose of supporting the title of this book, let's call it "Your Activation Map."

When looking at your system to create your map of activation, be sure to include eight key areas: self, family, purpose, career, finances, social, spiritual, and health/fitness aspects. This map should be a visual and written representation of your ideal "happy" life. Think of a vision board with a written action plan. This may seem like many things to consider, but if you look at each one and take a major life decision into consideration, you will begin to see how your life would be impacted in each key area. Stephen Covey, author of *The Seven Habits of Highly Effective People*, advises in his Habit #2 to start with the "end in mind." This is also a good principle to use when beginning to create your life map. By practicing Habit #2, you can have a clear vision of your desired direction and destination, and continually make adjustments as necessary to make it happen. This allows you to visualize who you are and what you want in life, and you can then empower other people and circumstances to guide you through your life map. This life map, if done correctly, should help you identify your core values, give you a clearer sense of purpose, increase self-motivation, improve your focus and academic/career achievements, manage stress more effectively, recognize self-limiting beliefs, identify your strengths and talents, and build better relationships. Most importantly, learn how to simply live your life to the fullest while thriving through life's transitions on your way to reaching your destination.

Dr. Ramona Hollie-Major

Contributors

Dee Marshall

Dee Marshall is regarded "a Coach whose name shows up on the short list of top Coaches for women." In a just a few years she went from being a credentialed Coach in private practice to a "renowned expert" for women, says *Essence* Magazine. She has built a women's empowerment empire to include several entities for women: Raise The Bar, LLC, Dee Marshall Etc., DeeCMarshall.com, ThePowerSuite.com, Girlfriends Pray, and Young Savvy.

She inspires, encourages, motivates, challenges, and supports women, and her brand umbrella reaches over 40,000 women around the world. To sum it up, her work goes above and beyond the two primary areas of expertise—life and business.

Monique Strachan-Murray

Monique Murray, Author, Speaker, Soldier of Love and empowerment specialist for teenage girls and young women. A native of Freeport Bahamas, Mrs. Murray is the creator of "The Redefining Project" and "Herstory" workshops designed for teenage girls and young women to have honest and focused conversations about Life, Self-Love and Relationships. She also the newly published author of book entitled "Soldier of Love." Her hope is to prevent a wounded teenage mindset from becoming a broken spirit in the future. Mentorship is what she thrives for and believes that it will help one to unlock their full potential, optimize their leadership skills and become Soldiers of Love! See more of Monique at www.healingwithintoday.com

Ramona Hollie-Major, EdD, MBA

Dr. Hollie-Major aka "The Co-Pilot" is a results-oriented leader, educator, coach, philanthropist, speaker, and writer. As a senior executive, she has coached and mentored both entry level and management level staff to realize their goals. She has a leadership approach that embodies developing the mind, body and spirit. Leadership Programs for Aspiring and New Leaders is her passion and Signature Series.

She is co-founder of Naked Truth Living. An organization dedicated to providing the Naked Truth of relationships both personally and professionally. We believe that Revealing, Healing & Inspiring is the foundation necessary to adequately equip and empower people for personal and professional growth. We want to serve as a resource for persuasive inspiration with the hope of realizing meaningful change and impactful growth in the lives of others.

Ramona enjoys spending time with her family and friends, traveling, spiritual and personal development, and serving God and her community. See more of Dr. Hollie at www.DrHollieMajor.com

Develop Your Own Thing

In order to activate in my life, I had to release other people's limitations and expectations of what I should do. There were times when I was too busy being worried about what other people thought of me and whether I was doing the right thing according to them.

To move forward, it was important that I sought motivation in a variety of positive places such as books, conferences, positive areas of social media, and circles where people of like mind were present. I believe it has changed my life, professionally and personally, and has also assisted in my overall development and building a system of support. Aside from that type of motivation, my kids are my biggest motivators now. This has created a newer foundation for our family and one for them to continually build upon. This has also catapulted me into stepping outside of my comfort zone and creating new opportunities for myself. I am setting the example.

My Core Message of Activation

Develop Your Own Thing! A lot of women have a passion that they do not tap into, get very comfortable working for somebody else, and find that they are very unhappy. I am not suggesting that you can't be happy at a full time job because I have one that I am extremely happy in. But I also have other desires and passions that I want to pursue outside of that. My core message is that every woman has a message and a passion and in some form or fashion she needs to tap into that and share it with the world.

Activation Steps

1. **Accept Yourself** – Don't focus on what is good or bad about you, but look at yourself as a work in process and accept all the parts of your story. This process helps you to walk in your purpose. Accept yourself, then ask for help, regardless of your level of success, and continue to grow, build, and learn.

2. **Settle into Your Passion** – Most passion comes from a painful past. Work on the healing, do the necessary therapy, and be willing to share your story and passion with the world.

3. **Stop Being Invisible and Become Visible** – You have something to say that your corner of the world needs to hear. I do it every day and it has helped me to help other women.

My moniker, the "global visibility expert, is what I do—I help people become visible globally whether it is their business, their brand, their message, or their personal identity. It was through self-discovery, therapy, and talking with friends that I figured out why I was so motivated to get things done. Find out what you are motivated to do and get it done! For whom? For you!

Just start doing it! Just start. A lot of us, self included, want the whole plan. We want to know the beginning, the middle, the end, but that is not how life works. We get so rooted in having to know the plan that we don't do anything to move forward, until we have it. So start and then the plan will unfold. We have to have faith, a support system, and the willingness to fail in order to be a success. We get so rooted in fear and the unknown that we don't even get started. The first step to activating your message, purpose, or dream is to JUST START. You can begin by reading these awesome stories.

Nikki Woods

Queendom

Building a Social Empire by Embracing Your Inner Royalty

Have you ever been told that you were not capable of achieving your dreams in life? Have you shared your dreams with those you love only to be told that you could not make it? And did you believe them because they love you and they think they know what's best for you? You therefore put your dreams on hold and continue living life the way you think you should be living based on what others are telling you. Well, let me tell you that you are capable of making your dreams come true, and I am living proof of this. When you truly believe in yourself, no matter what other people are saying, you can make your dreams become a reality. It is your life and you have the control, the power to live your dreams.

When I was in high school, I realized that my life was being controlled by my parents and by society. I was not living my own life. I was told to study hard, graduate from a top college, get a job, work my way up the corporate ladder, save money, have a family, and retire. You know, they tell you to study hard so that you can get a high-paying job and live happily ever after. If you look around in today's world, people are stuck. People no longer know how to fully live and enjoy life. People stay at jobs they hate because it pays the bills and they have forgotten about that dreams they once had.

I have always been a dreamer and I knew I was brought into the world to help and to inspire others. I was destined for greatness, to be someone important, not just a normal person in the busy world. It all started in high school when I knew that in order to achieve my dreams, I had to break away from society's norm and believe in myself.

I was born and raised in the San Francisco Bay area in California. I attended one of California's top 50 public high schools; where most students would go on to obtain their degrees from the University of California (UC's) system. My high school put an incredible amount of emphasis on academics and creating students to be "book smart" rather than "street smart." Students were so focused on and devoted to getting a 4.0 GPA and perfect SAT scores. As a student at Mission San Jose High School, I felt an unspoken rule that all that mattered was academics and continuing your education at a top UC or Ivy League school. You got good grades to make your parents proud. As a junior in high school, I realized that there was this bubble where all that seemed to matter was academics. Between high school and my life at home, I was extremely sheltered. My parents had full control of my life and I did not want to be a rebel because I did not want them to be disappointed in me, especially since I am the oldest daughter. But I knew there was so much more to explore in life, so much more to learn and experience, so when it came to researching colleges, I knew that I did not want to follow the crowd.

It was a childhood dream of mine to live and work in New York City. I knew it was not going to be an easy dream to pursue because my life was defined by what my family wanted for me. When you're seventeen years old, you believe in what people tell you because you don't know any better. So what did I do? I told myself that in order to live my dreams, I had to stop caring about what others said and do what was best for me. I knew that I wanted to have my own business one day in New York City, so I studied hard so that I would have the option of being accepted to colleges outside of California—specifically in New York. During my college search, I discovered Syracuse University which had a top-rated entrepreneurship program. It was close enough to New York City and I knew that was the stepping stone to pursuing my dreams. I knew that I wanted to be away from home in California and Syracuse University was my answer, my escape.

During high school, my family life was far from perfect. My sister is five years younger than me and always looked up to me as a role model. When I told her that I wanted to go away to New York for college, she felt like I was abandoning her to stay alone with our parents. I told her that with me in New York, if she didn't want to be in California she could always escape to New York to visit me if she wanted. I wanted to show her that parents will be parents because they care, but we still had full control over our lives. I needed to escape my family in order to pursue my dreams and what I wanted for myself. It might sound selfish, but I knew there was an entire world to explore and I had to do it on my own. My family was my motivation for doing everything necessary to make sure I was accepted at Syracuse University. I knew that in order to pursue my dreams, I had to leave California.

The day I received my acceptance letter from Syracuse University was one of the happiest days of my life. My prayer was answered and I knew this was only the beginning of a long journey ahead in pursuing my dreams. My family, especially my father, was so disappointed after discovering that I had only been accepted to two schools: Syracuse University in New York and the University of San Francisco, which was about forty minutes away from our home in Fremont. The only person in my family who would have the final say in which college I was to attend was my father. He was the one who was going to pay for my education and back then, I believed in everything he said. I prayed that my father would let me go to Syracuse and to this day, I believe that he allowed me to because he knew that being away from California would help me mature quicker. My high school mentor, Jaime Richards, promised me that he would look after my sister when I went away for college. Mr. Richards was the one person in high school who truly supported my dreams when no one else did, and to this day, he still supports me as he did when he first met me when I was seventeen years old.

August of 2008 was the beginning of my life away from California. My parents flew with me to Syracuse, New York to help me move into my college dorm. I remember looking out the small window in my single room, crying tears of joy and fear, as my parents drove off. I was free, independent, and ready for my new life. I was scared about the unknown, but I knew I was a step closer to my New York City dream. I was told I was crazy for wanting to go away and be away from family, yet there I was, a freshman at Syracuse University and ready to continue on my chosen path. It was at that moment I truly realized that I had full control over my life and I was capable of making things happen despite what everyone else said.

It was at Syracuse University that I discovered my love for social media marketing. This was where I found my inner social media royalty. It wasn't until my sophomore year that I entered my entrepreneurial studies and discovered my passion. I also noticed that my friends started calling me a "social media addict" because I was always on Facebook, Instagraming photos, and Tweeting away about everything. I then found myself really studying social media on a more professional level. Back then, the social media world was just beginning. I was involved in the Entrepreneurship Club at SU, where I held the VP of Marketing position during my junior year and was President my senior year. I realized that utilizing social media networks helped the club with membership and promotion of events. During my junior year, I also launched my first startup: *Check It!, LLC*, a mobile coat-checking business that would store the students' winter coats while they were out at the bars. This prevented expensive coats from being lost inside the crowded bar or stolen. As the VP of Marketing Director, I started to use Facebook and Twitter as a way to expose the business to SU students. Unfortunately, that business failed after a year but I did learn that social media marketing can help businesses. That was the exact moment when I realized that businesses can use social media marketing for exposure and to gain more customers. So I spent the last two years of my college education studying more about social media strategies for businesses.

I knew the next step of my dream was to move to New York City after graduating and taking all of my social media knowledge to help businesses. This was easier said than done. I applied to numerous entry-level positions at social media agencies in New York City, hoping to land a job so that I could work in NYC right after graduating. After applying to all those jobs, however, I wasn't hired at any of them because I lacked experience. I was feeling so discouraged and felt like I had failed myself because I couldn't get hired for the jobs that I wanted.

On top of that, my own family started to lose faith in me. My parents were so disappointed in me because I didn't have a job offer upon graduating. My dad told me he was disappointed in me and that after investing in my education, he wished he had never sent me away to Syracuse because he lost control over my life. However, I realized that by being away from California for four years, I transformed into a mature woman who didn't care about what others said because I was so driven to achieve my NYC dream.

So I made a deal with my dad. The deal was to give me a year to live on my own in NYC. If I couldn't figure it out on my own, then I would move back to California. He agreed and helped with me with my rent and expenses since I was a recent college grad. When I moved to NYC, I knew that I wanted to start my own social media company. I also knew that I needed to find a job first and have a steady income since NYC is one of the most expensive cities to live in. So I continued my job search while studying social media marketing. Two months after graduating, I was hired by a small company for a customer service position which also included some social media marketing. I accepted the offer immediately because I knew this was what I needed to help launch my business. The company was small and didn't feel too corporate, and it had an innovative side to it.

At the same time, I was introduced to the "Young Female Entrepreneurs of NYC" group in November 2012. This was where the *#SocialMediaQueen* was really born and stuck with me. I spoke with these women entrepreneurs and learned about their businesses. Most of them told me that they had no idea on how to use social media marketing or that they felt that social media was too overwhelming. That was my *AH-HA!* Moment.

This was my opportunity to focus on launching my own social media company. I continued working at my nine-to-five job while attending as many entrepreneurial events as I could. I wanted to work with small business owners. I also found myself as the person who tweeted and Instagram-ed the most at business events by using hashtags. I had discovered my niche and jumped on every business opportunity that presented itself.

In January 2013, I launched my company, "SV Consulting." I had my website and company logo created. Then I started branding myself as the #SocialMediaQueen and that really caught people's attention. I also made a promise to myself that I would become a full-time entrepreneur before my twenty-third birthday in October. In March 2013, I had my first paying client. It was all happening so fast.

In June 2013, I had a talk with my corporate boss. She kindly suggested that I start looking for other job opportunities because she wasn't sure about where my career was heading within this small company. She moved me from full-time to part-time at the company. I was so happy when she told me I would be working there only three days a week. That meant that I had more time to focus on my own business.

In July 2013, I met Lucinda Cross and started working on the social media campaign for the Activate Conference in September 2013. After meeting Lucinda, the doors flew wide open. So many entrepreneurs needed help with their social media marketing! I was making more money in my own business than from my part-time "corporate job." I realized that I no longer wanted to go in to work; it was draining my energy and I wasn't even doing social media, which is what I love doing. I knew I had to quit and devote my full attention to my growing business and my clients.

On September 4, 2013, I had my first speaking engagement with my powerful female entrepreneurs. That same morning, I quit my nine-to-five job, where I had worked for fourteen months. I will never forget the feeling I had when I stepped outside of that office. I felt so free! I was so proud of myself. I walked around and looked up at the city buildings, saying "thank you New York City." My childhood dream of living in NYC with my own business had turned into a reality. I believed in myself and I made it all happen. I took a leap of faith and the rest is history.

The Activate Conference in September 2013 was incredible. We were expecting 150 attendees and over 300 people showed up. I was amazed by the number of people who came up to me and introduced themselves. They would say, "Hey, you're Stephanie, the #SocialMediaQueen! I'm___ and I have been following you and I love what you are doing…" I remember that I was running around in this gorgeous mansion in Long Island, taking photos and tweeting everything with #Activate2013. I was also reposting what attendees were sharing throughout the day. It was one of the most amazing experiences of my life. I was doing what I loved!

Since the day I quit my nine-to-five job, my business has exploded. I have been working with private clients in managing their social media accounts. I have been working with business conferences and events. I've also been teaching social media courses both online and offline. I have met amazing business owners and am grateful to be connected in different networks across the country. I am grateful to cross paths with powerful women entrepreneurs, who understand me so well I call them my New York family. Being an entrepreneur is not easy; there will be times when you feel like quitting. The important thing is to have a support network to help you fight through life's struggles, especially when your loved ones don't quite understand what you're doing.

I am also thankful that my family in California has become more supportive of my dream and I love that I can visit whenever I want. Even my sister wants to help me with my business, which means a lot to me because I am always trying to be a good role model for her. After everything I have been through, I can inspire her and others by showing them it is possible to achieve your dreams. When you love what you are doing, it isn't a job. If you aren't happy with your situation, you have the power to change it. It is never too late to pursue what you love doing. You have full control of your life. I am living proof that anything is possible at any age. I hope my story as the #SocialMediaQueen will inspire you and others.

So now that you've read about my story in becoming the #SocialMediaQueen, you're probably wondering how to use social media marketing to build your own business.

Activate Your Social Media

As a business owner, you have to understand that social media marketing is not about your business; it's about understanding your audience and engaging in conversations with them. You should be using social media to capture people's attentions. Your social media pages should be unique and different from your competitors' pages. Your business pages should be consistent and brand-tight on social media. Your pages should also have a personal touch to it because people are connected to people who have the similar interests. First, people will become consumers, which means those who are following your social media pages will begin to learn about your business. You have to understand where your consumers are on social media and focus on growing those specific platforms, whether it's on Facebook, Twitter, Instagram, LinkedIn, etc. From there, consumers who trust you will become customers. Customers are people who purchase from your business, whether it's a product or a service.

Social media should be the doorway to gaining consumers. Once you have consumers, including followers and Facebook fans, they will turn into customers when they purchase from your website and invest in your business. The goal in posting content and sharing photos on social media is to provide value to your audience and engage in conversations. These conversations result in "likes," comments, shares, and followers. Once consumers find value in your social media pages, they will share it within their own networks and "talk" about you on social media. The power of social media marketing is in allowing you to connect with anyone in the world! There are so many ways to build your social media royalty, from participating in Twitter chats, Tele-summits, Google Hangouts, and so much more to showcase your expertise and products. Remember that the key to social media marketing is consistency, which will increase your social media royalty.

Stephanie Voong

Just Do You
Creating a Life of Enough

"You may not control all of the events that happen to you, but you can decide not to be reduced by them." –
Dr. Maya Angelou

As a young child, you are innocent with no worries in the world. At most, you are worried about not getting to play with Barbie dolls or play in the park, go ice-skating, eat ice cream, and the list goes on. Unhappy feelings are foreign to you unless you are crying for something that you want and your parents don't give it to you. As you grow older, you may start experiencing different feelings or emotions, which may seem foreign to you. They can be feelings of isolation, loneliness, and even low self-esteem. But where did they come from? Why do you feel this way, you may wonder? The next thing you may wonder is *"who can I turn to, who I can talk to about these feelings?"* When these questions go unanswered, then what happens?

From a young age, I remember being a very outgoing child. I loved to laugh, smile, sing (mostly at a yelling pitch), and enjoyed participating in school activities. But that came to an instant halt at the age of ten. I was entering the fourth grade, but this time I felt less confident about myself. My body looked different. I no longer "looked like everyone else." I put on a few extra pounds, and now felt like the chubby kid. I didn't get teased at school, luckily for me, but I did get teased from the people I expected to guard and protect me most: my family.

The word "fatty" become something I heard on a daily basis. This was the first time I experienced feeling a sense of isolation. Being shy became my new norm. As a young child, I had no clue about what to do. I never considered myself an overeater, but I did love candy, the most evil form being chocolate. Anything I could get my hands on involving chocolate was devoured in 2.5 seconds. I'm guessing you know what my favorite holiday was back in the day—Halloween! I digress a bit. My mom was slightly overweight, so I didn't have the best guidance in terms of why healthy eating was important, and what those foods consisted of. Instead, what I knew was being ridiculed about my eating without a solution.

I began to notice my light dim, and I no longer identified with being an outgoing child. That bright and vivacious kid had become hardened. I kept a lot of things to myself. On the outside I may have appeared to be fine, but deep down inside, I was hurting. I can say that I had what appeared to others to be a great childhood. My mom and dad took great care of my siblings and me. I went on great vacations and I generally got what I asked for, but I still always felt emptiness inside. I didn't feel "safe" to express my feelings. In my immediate family we looked out for each other, but I wouldn't say we were emotional and expressed our feelings. In fact, we rarely said "I love you," and no one talked about his or her issues. We just did our own things. I handled myself as best I could by pretending all was well, but this was the start of what I like to call my "daily inner battle." I was a young kid feeling like I needed to figure things out on my own.

When I attended family functions, like barbeques, those feelings were exacerbated. I experienced public scrutiny that made me always feel like all eyes were on me. I was always asked, "Oh, what do you have on your plate?" even though no one else was asked the same question. I would always brush it off with a snarky comment, but deep down inside, I was hurt. These instances didn't allow me to feel like I could just let myself "be." I was constantly reminded of the area I fell short of in my life – my health. My hardened heart transpired into an attitude of "Nothing bothers me," and "I got this; I don't need your help." Oftentimes I misconstrued situations as a direct attack to me because I had become highly sensitive. A part of me had died.

This became very evident in my earlier parts of high school. I remember focusing on the last thing that really mattered, which was being cool. I made sure I became friends with all the upperclassmen, I barely did any schoolwork—although I managed to get decent grades—and I was very critical of who I hung out with, oftentimes judging people based on how they looked instead of by their hearts. Midway through high school, I got a wake-up call, which I believed was from God, to get my act together. It was a faint whisper that said, "You are better than what you are portraying to the world." This ultimately led me to slowly change my ways. I had to think of my future, like how the heck I would get into college! I always wanted great things for myself but I couldn't get myself there. I began to do work and actually study, which I realized came very easily to me. In fact, I picked up haters VERY quickly. The ones who did well and were probably secretly judging me began to wonder: *How could someone go from barely doing anything to receiving A's on everything?* That one switch enabled me to feel alive for the first time. I began to seek out what I wanted for myself. I started to be an active player in my life. In fact, I went against what everyone else was doing in taking a foreign language as an elective. I have nothing against learning another language because I think that's great. However, when I had the opportunity to take a risk and jump into something different, I did. Instead, I took on business and computer classes, which I ended up loving. I began my quest to dig deeper into what I wanted to do. These shifts gave me the confidence to tackle my weight issues. I lost thirty pounds and went from a size twelve to a size six.

After graduating high school, I went off to college with a better outlook on life. During college, I became involved with many organizations and even became a part of a sorority, Alpha Kappa Alpha Sorority, Incorporated. What I noticed was that even with everything I was involved in; I still had the same old struggles, which ultimately manifested in wanting to feel like I was a part of something greater. Those around me never saw me as someone who struggled internally, but I did what I did best; I acted like everything was okay. Those same issues carried into how I treated people and the crew I kept around me. I don't view it as being as tortuous as it was when I was a child. However, there really was no personal growth in how I wanted to really feel and in how I treated others. The major shift for the worst took place when I entered corporate America. I stepped into a competitive environment (which I didn't think would be an issue since I'm competitive by nature) in which I had to work closely with folks of varying personalities, deal with office politics, and accept critiques on work performance. Those feelings of "am I good enough?" and "what do people think of me?" quickly resurfaced in a major way. I often found myself again battling a constant inner conflict. There were very specific moments when this turmoil emerged, such as when it came time to do presentations, which I was required to do quite often. Those moments were grueling for me. I was constantly stressed out and often sick, and soon I noticed the pounds piling on again.

There was a specific time that I remember like yesterday where I believe I let myself down. I was working at an assessment firm in a rotational program, which meant I had the opportunity to rotate into four different groups that supported various business lines (six months each track.) After each rotation, I had to deliver a presentation in front of senior management and other team members who were often five to six level levels higher than my status. Yikes! Now you may be thinking that I tanked during the first one, but that actually happened during the last one. Yes, I already presented three times before, so it should have gotten easier for me, right? Well, nope! As I looked up at the screen and saw my presentation pop up, I knew it was my time to go. I was looking sharp – hair done, nice suit, and shoes on point, but where was my confidence? I walked up to the podium and my heart was racing so fast I thought I was going to pass out. I remember speaking so fast because I just wanted to sit back down. After I was done, the audience clapped but I'm sure it was only because they wanted to be polite. I knew deep down inside that I hadn't given my best. What I realized is that I had put too much pressure on myself simply because it was my last presentation in my program. I also started bringing up the past feelings of wondering if it was good enough, how I could make it perfect, and if people would like me and the content of my presentation.

What was strange to me was that although I had a desire to be a great speaker, I often ran from it. When I watched management give stellar presentations, I would often say, "That's going to be me; I'm going to be one of the top presenters." Instead, I let my fears guide my actions. In other cases, I would make up excuses for why a presentation should be postponed or I'd do it at the very last minute. Last-minute practicing meant I wasn't confident, and I would constantly question if I had given it my all. This resulted in a vicious cycle of self-torment. What I noticed during all of these incidents is that the old lies I used to tell myself just kept resurfacing, and that what I used to tell myself wasn't true. Why? Because I never allowed myself to talk about how I felt inside, this would just continue to manifest in different ways.

Luckily for me, through working at an investment bank, I began to work on my ways slowly but surely. The next time those feelings came across again was when I didn't receive a promotion that I should have gotten. When I asked senior management about it, the response I got was that I was doing a great job and that it was an oversight. I was ready to write down my areas of improvement only to be greeted by blank stares. I have to admit, those feelings of being alienated and not thinking I was good enough crept right back up. This time, it manifested into extreme anger and to make matters worse, I was studying for a professional certification exam, Series 7, so between feeling like I wasn't being appreciated and clearly not in the "in crowd," the "I don't care attitude" took full effect. Within four to five months, I gained about thirty pounds. This time, I clearly knew I was reaching for things that I shouldn't, like alcohol, cookies, and brownies. It was the perfect combination for gaining tons of weight. I just didn't care about anything, including myself, and that clearly showed on my body. Luckily, I had already decided in my head that it was time to leave this job because my unhappiness wasn't worth the anxiety, plus I knew deep down inside that it wasn't my passion. So I left to rebuild my health, to work on myself, and to gain back my sanity. Shortly after, I started my own company and I'm now in a much better place. It took a long time for me to accept my greatness and to know that I earned every great thing that happened in my life.

Your situation may look different than mine. For me, the issue was being overweight as a child and allowing the projection of others to torment me. For you, it may be different, but your struggles may be the same. I wish I knew how to fully enjoy my life. So many years of my life were not enjoyable due to the torment that I brought on myself. I used to secretly give my mom the side-eye, as if to question why she didn't help me back then. But what I realized is that because she was overweight herself, she wasn't in the best position to help me. She needed to help herself before she could help me. So those feelings I used to harbor towards her I've since let go. I'm in a better place today because I invested in personal development and in tools to help me be my best self.

Today I can thankfully say that I'm operating with purpose and passion. I always knew deep down inside that God was preparing me for something bigger than I could imagine. That prompted me to save up for my exit (whenever that time presented itself) and I also enrolled in a nutrition school. Even though I excelled in my corporate career, I was extremely unhappy. I reached a point where I could barely get out of the bed in the morning. I debated for a year and decided to take the leap of faith and leave corporate America to start my own company, *Unhealthy No More*. I teach busy professional women to thrive at work and in life by creating nutrition and wellness plans specific to their lifestyles. I also emphasize that healthy living isn't all about fitness and eating healthy, but also about nurturing the mind and making time for spiritual practices.

I'm writing for major publications, speaking at corporations, and I'm helping people live their best lives, which I enjoy. I now take the time to celebrate my accomplishments and myself. I'm bold enough to declare what I want and go after it. I now believe in myself and my abilities to be the bold, confident, and courageous woman God destined for me. A constant reminder for me is, "God hath not given me the spirit of fear, but of love and of power and of a sound mind" (2 Timothy 1:7 KJV).

You have one life to live. Be happy, conquer all, fail and get back up, love, and enjoy, because life is short. If you change what you say and think about yourself, the right things will come to you. What you say, you become. Be kind to yourself and get the help and guidance that you need to jump over that mountain and be your best self.

If being overweight is an issue that has stopped you from being the best you can be, has hindered you from pursuing your dreams, or you are carrying around a lot of emotional baggage, here are a few action steps you can take to help you reach your goals.

Activation Steps

Your "Why" — Write down why you want to lose weight and get healthy. It could be because you don't have energy to play with your kids, you want to feel more confident about how you look, have better self-esteem, or perhaps you haven't pursued your dreams because your weight has been holding you back.

When you figure it out, make sure you post it everywhere you'll be tempted (ahem … at work, your refrigerator, your car… you get the point!). Get really specific, write it down, and dig deeper!

Listen to Your Body — Take time to learn what your body likes and doesn't like. What is good for one person may not be the right answer for you. Your body knows what it wants and does not want. Once you remove the foods that don't make you feel good, you will be more likely to stay on track. Food journaling is a great option for identifying which foods are right and wrong for your body.

Accountability — If there are people who are not supportive of your health goals, reduce the quantity of time you spend with them and don't look to them as people to uplift you during your journey. Get an accountability buddy who will keep you in check. When you have cheerleaders rooting for you, you are more inclined to succeed in reaching your health goals. Surround yourself with positive energy! Look to those people who truly support you to keep you grounded.

Gratitude journal — Keep a gratitude journal and every day (top of the morning or before you go to bed) list out three things you are thankful for. When you exercise gratefulness, you can expect the following benefits: peace and calmness, noticing what's good in your life, healing your emotional wounds, feeling blessed, and finding that even the smallest things will bring you joy.

Spiritual practice — Develop a spiritual practice. Health and wellness isn't one-dimensional. It's more than what you put in your mouth. You want to ensure you are grounded and have an outlet that keeps you calm. When you feel unfilled, this can lead you to destructive behaviors involving food. Maybe your idea of spirituality is prayer, reciting positive affirmations, or meditation. Whichever spiritual vehicle you choose, be sure to schedule times for regular reflection throughout your day.

List out your fears — Get out a piece of paper and write out all of your fears or insecurities. This exercise will help you to make a connection between your fears and your reality. When you look at your list, I want you to ask yourself: *Is this really true? What truth is really behind it?* Then I want you to reframe what you said and speak the truth about yourself. For example, if you say, "It's impossible for me to lose weight," or "My life is not worth living," "or "I can't be confident," is that really true? Or is it something you were led to believe or convinced yourself of?

Vanessa Cunningham

Quiet Storm
Silence Can Be the Silent Killer

Have you ever felt like you were going through life merely existing? Are you desperately searching for a way to connect your internal and external self, hoping to find wholeness? I get it; I have been there! You might be thinking *I have so many flaws; I am so fragmented, how will I ever integrate all of me to become the best person that God created me to be?* Maybe this feeling stems from the messages provided to you by family, society, or your own perceptions of them.

What fuels you to continue moving forward is that desire to connect and assimilate all of who you are. There is a part of you that is actually aware on some level that your existence in this world is formed by more than atoms and neurons. You are not the first woman to be at this crossroads of life or to have the inability to speak your truth and be authentic in every aspect without shame and guilt. But my prayer and desire for this chapter and this book is that you will be the last woman to live in a place of uncertainty and fear. The corporate evolution of women taking a stand, finding their voices and uniting will create a surge of never-before-witnessed declarations.

You have done the "why me, God?" questions, blamed others for your trials, and even rationalized why others were better off than you. However, you came to the realization that wanting to create sustainable change and reinventing your former self will take work. Meditating, praying, speaking daily affirmations or even "speaking life" into your circumstances are all good disciplines and should be done. However, you are going to have to get down and dirty in the "stuff" that has perpetuated this existence. Your "stuff" may include broken dreams, unattained goals, failed relationships, or trial after never-ending trial.

You will not be walking away from just self-help, empowering story; rather, you will leave running with an excitement and energy to take on the world. No longer will the silence of your yesterday be invited into your today and tomorrow.

Please do not believe for one minute that I came out of my mother's womb with the tenacity for this way of thinking. Trust me when I say this has been work and is still a work in progress. But my journey has taught me that what I believe is what will manifest. It's a simple concept, but goes much deeper than we give it credit for.

Like me, you may have found yourself at some point with great distaste for yourself. You may have found yourself without a voice or feel like you are unworthy of a platform from which to speak your truth. So, what do I want for you and what do I hope you want for yourself? If you are TRULY ready, I want you to be receptive and comfortable with being uncomfortable and with being vulnerable. I want you to discover the innate beauty that exists within you. I want you to know with every fiber of your being you are worth being in the presence of God and worth the presents promised by Him.

Take a deep breath and scan your emotional and mental self. What are the thoughts that enter your conscious state? What is your physical self exhibiting at this very moment? Are you feeling tension throughout your body? Does your heart feel like its racing? What is occurring in the physical self is directly related to the mental and emotional self. Even when you are not actively thinking about "the wrongs of life," you would be surprised about how they manifest in your daily decisions and behaviors. Pay attention to those physical feelings. Remain cognizant as the problems and pains are replaced with purpose and passion.

Remember this is a journey! You may have great intention to go barreling to your anticipated destination. By all means, run. Run with fire and determination to create your new self. Be the one who does not apologize for her existence and celebrates every pre-destined step. However, also be aware that you may have a setback. Do not despair; this too is a part of your journey, and any lessons obtained during this period are beneficial to you. Just DO NOT get stuck in this space. Evaluate your growth and honor what you have accomplished and use those tools to foster continued forward movement.

It has taken me a great deal of work to be okay with shedding my "skin." For many years, I did not allow most people to get past the surface layer of who existed within me. I was always concerned that I would say or do the wrong thing. I felt like I wasn't good enough and if people knew my insecurities, they would dismiss me from their "circle." So, after years of hiding behind the strong, got-it-all-together façade, I realized the only circle that I am meant to be a part of that would glorify the best in me as well as accept my worst is "God's Circle." It was only then that I was able to feel comfortable with people knowing the real me and still walk with my head not just high, but very high. I had formerly been angry and bitter, hating everything and everyone, including myself. But in my defense, I felt that my story or rather the first half of my journey justified my brokenness. Since I know that you have already started the journey to healing (why else would you be reading this book?), you know that defense was debunked. What I am now aware of is the fact that my journey is not by chance, nor was it determined by some set of unexplainable events. My journey, my authentic truth, is meant to be a composition of my greatest lessons.

When I was a young child, my parents wanted the absolute best for me. As first-generation immigrants who saw great opportunities for their American-born child, they provided all I could ever want at my fingertips. But it all began with a good education, so that is what I got. However, going to the private school that my parents selected, the one that would give me a great fighting start would also be the beginning of my demise into silence. It was during this time that my babysitter's uncle saw my childhood innocence and my laughter and mistook it for adult companionship. It was the first of many unfortunate circumstances.

It's unfortunate that this person didn't see me for the little girl that I was, who simply wanted to play hopscotch and jump double-dutch. Human beings diligently work to fulfill the idea of self-preservation; therefore, this moment in time (which was more like two years) was removed from my consciousness. I placed these memories into the deepest and darkest place within my being. Apparently, I was aware that I was not ready to handle the reality of this life-changing event. However, nothing is truly withheld from the conscious state. Traumatic events remain in the very cellular level of existence, and all behavior that seems unspeakable and without reason is actually with great cause. But I wondered how it was possible to be so broken and depleted of all self-love before I had an opportunity to love life?

My knowledge of my role as a girl from that point was skewed. I yearned for love, acceptance, and belonging. If you have flashing red lights and sirens going off in your head as you read this, it's because you already recognize that things would get a lot worse for me before there was hope of getting better. The problem with this unspoken, untreated, and unrecognizable memory coupled with low self-esteem and self-worth is that every creepy and vile man on earth is able to recognize you. Like a dog smells fear on its prey, so do abusers, sexual harassers, and the like.

My silence was painfully loud, but it seemed like nobody could comprehend my way of speaking. My behaviors reeked of a shattered little girl screaming, begging to be saved. The only person that heard and knew exactly what I thought I needed was a neighborhood boy. At fourteen years old, I entered into a relationship that was as toxic as bleach, ammonia, and rat poison in a cocktail. But you could not tell me that I was not in love; you could not tell me that I would not marry and bear this person's children. You simply could not tell me anything that was not in line with the "greatness" of this relationship. He loved me for me; I didn't have to pretend to be smart, and I did not have to act like I was perfect or like my life was on display for approval. What I did have to do was mind my mouth or else I risked getting punched in the face. I gave the very essence of myself to him.

When my mother found out about this life that I had created for myself, she was mortified. However, I was so caught up in the dark wilderness; I truly could not see where I was going. She earnestly tried to talk me out of my choices, but I would not hear it. She just didn't understand—I was in love. I was in love with a boy who was not in school, sold drugs, and carried a gun. I mean, seriously, I could give my girlfriends the best advice, but be totally blind to my own DEVASTATION, DESTRUCTION, and DELAYS.

Thankfully, my journey does not end there. In the years following, there was the good, the bad, and the in-between. But finally, enough was enough. I knew that in order for my story to change, in order for my voice to be audible, I had to be an active participant in finding a solution. I needed to leave my "broke-through" mentality in the past and seek out a break-through in the present. No longer would I purposely sabotage my healing and growth. Notice I said purposely—and yes, I mean that. It would be easy to say that I was unaware of the actions that caused my abyss. Truth be told, I knew; I just did not care or love myself enough to do anything differently.

Resiliency is a concept that completely escapes science. How can two people go through similar walks and have varying outcomes? How does one person use her obstacle as the stepping stones to new opportunities, while another dwells in the "woe is me" state? I am no longer silent about any aspect of this journey of mine. The unification of mind, body, and soul and its great value to me and my God has created a woman who celebrates her trials. I honor the gifts of love, purpose, and faith.

What I have been blessed to understand is that we are equally privileged to accept the gifts that God has designed for our specific walks. However, it is up to each person to receive them. You say, "Life hurts and it's *so* hard to get past the fear, strife, and mayhem." Here's the problem with that mindset, according to 2 Timothy 1:7 KJV "For God did not give us a spirit of fear, but of power, love and a sound mind." Therefore,

YOU and I were not designed to live in a place of poverty. Our spiritual, physical, emotional, and financial selves were meant to be held in high regard. Whenever you desire that high regard more than anything else, you will start to do the things that are completely outside of your norm. The words "comfort zone" will equate to having your spleen pulled out without anesthesia.

So, ladies, what does all this mean? This means that life will be hard; life can and will hit you with some detours. You will have those moments thinking "I wish I had…", but here's the thing; we can't go back, and we can't alter the events that have led us to where we stand today. What we can do is revisit and re-evaluate those events that were not nurturing and, like a sequel to a movie, change the script for a different and greater future.

You may be saying to yourself, "Please, what does she know? Her stuff pales in comparison to mine. She couldn't even understand my walk. She does not know how heavy my burdens are. She just does not know." And you're right! My journey is different than yours and yours from the next woman's. But we do have a few things in common. We are each a mighty force and God has given us the keys to freedom. We ARE our sister's keeper. Do not look at this title as a chore, because it is an honor for me to be my sister's keeper, to lend an ear, give a hand, or offer a shoulder.

This is not reality TV. Your life is not scripted to make ratings. And you most definitely cannot filter what comes from your lips to pacify the masses. You have to live your truth if you are to start the healing process. Speak it, write it, and just get it out by any means necessary! We must change our perception of the world and the experiences we receive. In doing so, we will obtain the confirmation that we have created a new realm.

Unfortunately, we tend to wait for the suggestion that things have changed before we put forth the effort to change our mindset. It was only when I accepted vulnerability, rejected fear, and acknowledged my new reality that healing began. It may take time. It may take various formats, multiple people, and a wide range of circumstances, but when you keep PUSHING forth and making every effort, you will finally be receptive to God's blessings.

As previously stated, I am no longer silent. If you have an ear, I will share and do my duty as a child of the Most High to give my testimony of overcoming the obstacles that have presented themselves in my life. My current understanding of challenges are DISTRACTIONS attempting to separate me from my purpose. Fortunately, I have procured the four steps that make handling such hindrances a thing of the past. Be warned; it will be gut-wrenching work if you are truly honest with the process.

ACTIVATE

WHOOT WHOOT! You know what you want and you know why you want it, but are not certain about how to get the process started on this road to self-discovery, self-love, and self-growth. Simply stated, you must A.R.I.S.E. in love, faith, and vulnerability by following these steps:

ACCEPT - Accepting yourself with all your flaws and all the past shame/guilt and fears that haunt you and keep you awake. Accept yourself with all of your achievements and great contributions to your community. Accept yourself for who you know you are and not what society has claimed you to be. There are certain elements, like gender and skin color that cannot be changed, but everything else is potential waiting to be unleashed. All that encompasses "YOU" is an acceptable "YOU." You will know the precise moment when you are capable of ACCEPTING yourself. It will be when you have disrobed the belief system that has imprisoned you; it will be when you are yelling from the mountaintops with no inhibitions; it will be when you are the authentic, 100% you. It will also be when you tell everyone around you to jump off if they do not like what they see and hear, because you please your higher self—BAM!

1. Speak/Write daily affirmations and place them around you to have constant reminders of your acceptance of self.

2. Stay prayed up. Unfortunately, the messages handed down by family, media, and society can contribute to the negative viewpoints of self. Allow God to hand down His perfect messages to you!

3. Solicit people who are standing in their truth and have created their platform to be in your circle. Like-minded people will instill positive messages that will help you get to your acceptance platform.

4. See and be the change you do not find. If you don't find a group that fits your needs, create one. There is always someone that will benefit from your efforts. Small ponds create big waves.

RESPECT - Respecting yourself with the knowledge that you are a child of God and that any and all who approach you must honor His anointed with the highest of regard. Create standards for yourself that speak to your highest self. Your dress, your speak, body language… everything you do indicates the respect that you have for yourself and also lets the world know the level of respect that they MUST approach you with. If God respects you and the purpose you serve in this life, how dare anyone come at you with anything less!

Examine yourself and what you are showing the world. Petition trusted members of your community to assist you in this. You may be surprised at the responses, but take all that you receive as the brick and mortar needed to create the foundation for the new you.

IMPROVE ~ Improving yourself should be a constant. The belief system separating the "*haves*" and the "*have-nots*" is the idea that the learning process stops. Everything in life is a learning possibility. Go back to school; learn pottery, accounting, or tae kwon do. Learn how to be an entrepreneur or be the best mechanic. When you negate the learning process from life, you fall into a steady decline of "living." You are never too smart, too rich, too old, too *anything* to learn and improve yourself.

SELF-EVOLVE ~ While you are ACCEPTING, RESPECTING AND IMPROVING yourself, you are most definitely SELF-EVOLVING. It is inevitable that your transformation is in the making. You may not immediately recognize it. You may even wonder if you are becoming your higher self. But one day, you will look back and realize your friends are no longer the same people, you have made major contributions to your community, you have learned too many things to list, and you have jumped out of your comfort zone (in fact, your comfort zone likely no longer exists). You are on your way and those still around recognize the new you that is and continues to evolve!

Here is your first belief system: "fear and faith can't dwell in the same place." When you speak your faith, fear is drowned into silence. Speak boldly without any inhibitions. You are anointed and appointed for such a time as this. There is someone needing to hear your story and be inspired. Don't let them down!

Karen Poyser

Contributors

Nikki Woods

Nikki Woods, the bestselling author of Easier Said Than Done, is a multimedia personality, Social Media and Personal Branding Coach, Motivational Speaker, Voice-over Artist, and the CEO of Nikki Woods Media. She is also the senior producer of the acclaimed, nationally-syndicated Tom Joyner Morning Show (TJMS), the most successful syndicated urban radio show in history, reaching more than 8 million people on a daily basis. See more of Nikki at www.nikkiwoodsmedia.com

Stephanie Voong

Stephanie Voong is the *#SocialMediaQueen* of SV Consulting, a social media marketing firm that provides a variety of social media services for small businesses across the country. With a dual degree in Entrepreneurship and Marketing from Syracuse University, Stephanie knows social media is a powerful marketing tool that businesses need to understand and utilize to reach their fullest potential. She believes that social media marketing is important because it allows businesses to connect with people online before they even become customers and make purchases. See more of Stephanie at and SV Consulting at www.stephanievoong.com.

Vanessa Cunningham

Vanessa Cunningham is a Huffington Post contributor, nutrition and wellness expert of Unhealthy No More, Inc., author, and speaker based in New York City. A graduate of Pace University, she also studied at the Institute of Integrative Nutrition, where she was trained in more than 100 dietary theories and learned a variety of practical lifestyle coaching methods. She helps busy professional women prioritize their health by creating customized plans that are fun, sustainable, and easily integrated into their lifestyles. Through her holistic one-on-one coaching programs, dynamic workshops, and scintillating blog posts, she empowers her clients to thrive both at work and in life.

Her expert advice can also be seen on Essence.com, MommyNoire and MindBodyGreen. Her adoring fans have called her a "tell it as it is coach" and a "transformational coach." And when she's not teaching busy professionals how to live a balanced life and fit healthy living into their hectic schedules, you can find her indulging in self-help books, hanging out with her friends in NYC, or with her family in Long Island. See more of Vanessa at www.unhealthynomore.com

Karen Poyser

Karen Poyser-Navratil is a Licensed Clinical Social Worker (LCSW), whose focus includes, but is not limited to trauma, self-esteem, and depression. Karen has earned 3 degree of Bachelor's in Business Administration, a Master's in Public Administration (MPA) and a Master's in Social Work (MSW). Because of her love for the learning process, and her desire to grow and be the best for the teen girls and women she comes in contact with; she obtained a life coach certification from Florida International University. Karen is the CEO/ Founder and primary psychotherapist at A.R.I.S.E. (Accepting, Respecting, Improving and Self Evolving) One Support Services, LLC. Karen is a wife and mother of three daughters. And above all this, she is a child of God with purpose and passion who has walked through the pain! See more of Karen at www.ariseone.com

Action

In order to move forward, I had to release my past. Not just snippets or pieces, but all of it. I had to release all the things I put in my head, other people's voices in my head who told me that I couldn't do something. I had to release the should 'ves, the must 'ves, and the I have tos. I had to let go of my inner critic. My inner critic has served me well at times, because it forced me to do better. However, I wasn't happy because the harsh critic was taking over in my head and I really needed to listen to my heart. When I began to listen to my heart, I became more kind and gentle with my entire self.

It's always been hard for me to rely on or depend on other people. I seek motivation everywhere…books, CDs, conferences, speakers. I always sought motivation because I was looking for something or someone to say the right thing to motivate me. I have embraced and invested a lot of money in mentorship, community, and masterminding. I believe it's very important to connect with people who are like-minded and those who support you.

Seeking motivation is a great thing but I had to learn how to chew the meat (knowledge and wisdom) of what I was learning, spit out the bones (things not relevant), and not become fixated on (attending conference after conference) and searching so hard for certain answers. I soon found that I was hearing the same thing over and over again. Also, I found that I had to implement what I had learned and couple it with the drive inside of me. Finding the latter was my turning point to moving forward even further.

My Core Message of Activation

ACTION is the answer! If you are feeling stuck, it is because you're either not taking action or you are taking action that is not aligned with what you want to do and who you really are. Action is everything! Without it you have nothing but stagnation. I realized from working with many clients that lack of action is the main issue for many. I have been on a crusade to share that message with as many people as possible.

Activation Steps

1. **Take Action!** When you look back, you will be surprised by how much you've accomplished.
2. **Control Your Impulses!** Be patient with self and definitely with others. Everyone is not going to work within your timeline and everything doesn't need to happen overnight.
3. **Stop Making Excuses!** No matter how you package it or how reasonable it sounds, it's still an excuse. Be courageous and move forward.

This next set of stories will help you to take action and move forward.

Vasavi Kumar

Cut the C.R.A.P and Become Unstoppable!

"I'm not ready!" I heard myself say. I could feel my heart pounding against my ribcage with the force of bulls being held at the rodeo gate. My hands were wet with sweat and the last time I felt so nauseous was on a cruise ship being tossed about on the waves of the Atlantic. But there was no water here: only me and the sea of people who were waiting for me—and the nine other finalists—to take the stage.

Covered in hives, my right arm was itching beneath the lining of my crisp blue suit. It was over a hundred degrees outside in the brutal heat of the Dallas, Texas summer. So, even if I'd wanted to remove my jacket…I couldn't. It was as if my body was confirming the doubts that assaulted my mind. I didn't belong there!

It was the eWomenNetwork's very first North America's Next Greatest Speaker semi-finals. Out of over 1,000 speakers, I'd made it to the top 10. Earlier in the day, I'd met the other nine speakers during sound check. I was fine until I'd heard snippets of their polished and perfectly timed speeches. Every instinct in me wanted to run from the conference hall and never come back.

Fifteen minutes before the semi-finals started, I found myself in the middle of a meltdown. I'd tried to calm my nerves by running through my speech with my sister and manager, Gessie. But my mind went completely blank as I tried remembering the opening poem. Even though I'd written it, my mind refused to let the words spill out of my mouth.

That was the last straw. I finally snapped and asked my sister the question that had been plaguing me for the past couple of hours. I looked into her eyes and gave voice to the fears. "What the hell am I doing here?" I asked. The panic I heard in my voice scared me; it came straight from the core of my soul. I knew the question went deeper than the moment. It was one I was used to because I'd dealt with it most of my life—feeling I wasn't enough for the task ahead of me.

All my life, I battled the "not enoughs." I never felt smart enough, pretty enough, good enough, worthy enough—for anything that mattered to me. Most people never knew it, because if you back me into a corner, I will come out fighting. And, like makeup, I applied the mask of confidence every day.

I survived a seven-year depression that plagued me during my teens and early twenties. I am no stranger to working through my doubts and coaching my emotions…but this wasn't a normal moment. I was about to walk out on a stage in front of hundreds of people and tell them that I thought I was a speaker worthy of being called North America's Next Greatest Speaker (NANGS). But I felt as far from that title as the Earth is from the moon.

"I just need a moment and some quiet!" I told my sister. I closed my eyes and did all I know how to do when in a crisis. I prayed. I asked God to just help me make it through my speech. I'd already been told that I was sixth in the line-up. I just needed the strength of mind to hold on. I didn't need to win…I just needed to make it through!

I closed my eyes and counted, slowing my breath down to a pace that walked alongside my mind. "It's for you," I heard Gessie say, as she passed me her cell phone. I heard our youngest sister's voice on the end of the line. "Listen to me. I can tell you're nervous. But God wants me to tell you that your whole life has been preparation for this moment. You weren't meant to practice; everything happened just as it should. Just breathe. Go out on that stage and let God use you!" she said.

My spine straightened. I felt calm seeping into the spaces that were unraveling just moments earlier. Screaming mind chatter tuned down to a whisper. I realized then that the moment wasn't about winning. There was no competition. Whether or not I was good enough, this was ***my*** moment. It was a great opportunity and I needed to show up for it. As I walked backstage, I had only one thought. God had given me a "three-minute–opportunity" to touch others' lives and I was going to take it!

I made it to the top three that night and two days later, I would be crowned eWomenNetwork's first North America's Next Greatest Speaker. It is an honor that still humbles me, because I know the journey that led me to that stage.

Twenty-four years stood between the depressed teenager I used to be and the night of the NANGS semi-finals. It was years of personal development, work, and learning. Even after I was emotionally healthier, I didn't know how to live from a new place. I'd developed the habit of shrinking and playing small. I mastered being a wallflower that stayed out of everyone's way!

Over time, I'd transformed from a timid and depressed college student into a woman who dared to share her voice on stage in front of thousands. I once hid from my own shadow and now I seek to shine my light. How did I go from feeling as if life was pointless to the place where I know it is my divine appointment to empower others to live full out?

The answer is simple, but complex all at the same time. I was able to transform my life as I evaluated the attitudes, people, and mindsets that held me back, and I quickly realized it was C-R-A-P! Conquering mediocrity and moving forward requires us all to deal with the CRAP that threatens to derail us. That CRAP consists of:

- **C**ynics
- **R**egrets
- **A**pathy
- **P**eople Pleasing

As a Certified Empowerment Coach™, I work with high-performing women and men every day, helping them work through the mind chatter that tells them they are "not enough" to live their dreams in order to maximize their potential as business leaders and entrepreneurs, on and off the stage.

Together, my clients and I uncover the blocks that have kept them stuck in their careers, relationships, and other circumstances that don't serve them in their pursuit for greatness. I have coached hundreds of people and it is clear that CRAP keeps people universally stuck! We are all a work in process and in order for us to get the most out of life and work; we have to be willing to cut the CRAP.

DEALING WITH LIFE'S CYNICS:

Growing up, when a shoving match started on the playground, I would hear the childhood rhyme, "Sticks and stones may break my bones, but words will never hurt me!"

Children focused on keeping physical confrontation at bay bought into one of the most dangerous lies in society. Words have power that can do more harm than fists and knives!

Broken arms, legs, and other body parts can heal in a relatively short period of time. But poison-filled words can cripple a person from childhood to the grave. Everything begins with words. They are the foundation for life. The words people use in our environment matter. The danger of the cynic is that few recognize the damage done by their words.

Cynics are poisonous. They are toxic to everything we want to build in life. Unlike skeptics, who question things and merely need convincing, cynics have already made up their minds. By definition, they have lost hope in human potential for good. They don't believe in you and this makes it impossible for them to invest support in your dreams. A cynic's focus is singular—to prove that his or her negative view of the world is right.

When we are attempting to achieve anything great in the world, we must surround ourselves with possibility thinkers who see life with faith. Faith is not a hopeless attachment to fantasy; rather, it is the belief that there are options and solutions beyond the obvious.

Cynics can keep us from being in action. Unchecked, their poison and influence will spread. Before you know it, your dreams and passions have been infected. Dealing with a cynic at the work place or in social circles is a chore; however, it is even more painful when the cynic is a family member. But even then we have the right to choose who we hold in our confidence and heart space.

THE PSYCHOLOGY OF REGRET:

By the time I completed my Master's degree, my student loan debt was sizable. But I have never regretted the investment in my education—not even one day. For me, it was worth the price because I grew from the experience in ways that have made me a better person in every area of my life.

Many times, we get stuck because of our focus on past mistakes. Too much time and energy can be spent lamenting things that cannot be changed. In the field of psychology, there is an area of study known as the psychology of regret that focuses on the effects of regret on our lives.

Many of us have made serious missteps in life and long for the opportunity to do things differently. But in truth, it is our mistakes that have made us into who we are. We are only capable of different behavior because of the things we regret.

I understand my worth as a woman, because I've been the "friend" on the other end of the line telling someone how he deserves better than the woman in his life. I know how to walk away from toxic relationships, because I've had to rebuild my soul from being around critical people who couldn't love themselves—let alone find the time to value what was in me.

Research also shows that most regrets aren't centered around mistakes we've made; they stem from the actions that we failed to take! Standing backstage for the semi-finals, I literally felt as if my life was in a whirlwind. But I know that if I'd never entered the competition, I would have spent the rest of my life wondering what would've happened if I did? If I'd sat on the sidelines and watched everything unfold, I would have always wondered if it could have been me. Now, I know that it could be me…because it was me!

It can be easy to simply say, *"Let it go!"* But the art of release is more challenging than the theory. In order to cut the CRAP that comes from regret, we must deal with regret.

It's okay to make mistakes. It's okay to screw things up. It is okay to fall down and feel like you can't get up. It is just a feeling. Stabilize yourself and get back to life. As long as you're moving forward…it doesn't matter if you're walking or limping towards your dreams. Be in movement.

APATHY IS PATHETIC:

Apathetic people don't inspire change—at least, not for the good. We only need to walk the hallowed halls of history to discover that any movement that significantly impacted the course of a people or a nation came at great cost. Martin Luther King Jr., Winston Churchill, Sojourner Truth, and most of all, Jesus Christ…they all had to put skin in the game.

The danger of disappointment and failure is that it can drain your passion. And a sad but true fact about life is that the people who need you the most tend to hurt you the deepest. The temptation then becomes to simply throw in the towel and abandon the relationship.

If we're not careful, we become numb and calloused. We get tired of the hurt and pain. So we instinctively withdraw in an effort to protect ourselves from more of the same. But that effort to protect can quickly debilitate into a state of emotional numbness. It is dangerous to stop caring!

If your vision, passion, or relationship doesn't move or inspire you, it won't touch anyone else either! There will be moments in life when everything else fails, but if you still care… you will recover! You will find the way, you will endure, and you will outlast and outsmart adversity.

We must guard our hearts on a daily basis by taking inventory over what we allow to influence us. If we pick up offenses, they will cut us off from our destiny and the results we desire to experience.

The only way to do this is to keep your vision clear and in focus. Always remind yourself of why you do what you do! Understanding that will keep you fueled, even when the people you want to help don't get it.

PEOPLE PLEASING:

Despite our best efforts to get along with everyone, there will always be breakdowns. We can't allow the pursuit of acceptance and approval to set the standard for our actions. We are at our most ineffective point when the goal of our pursuits is approval and acceptance from others. If we allow others to dictate how we feel about ourselves, we will never have the courage to take ownership of own lives.

We can't control how others see us. Because people don't always see us for who we are they see us through whom they are. Their past and experiences color their interpretation and reality. We are at our most powerful when we simply dare to express our uniqueness.

If we are more concerned with making others comfortable with our decisions, choices, and personalities, then we will never tap into our unique brilliance and master the things essential to the fulfillment of our destinies.

GET YOUR SCISSORS OUT:

I know what it is like to stand at the edge of destiny, believing in your heart that life truly has more to offer than you've ever experienced. But transformation requires more than belief, hope, and inspiration. It is the result of taking action!

As you pursue your dreams, you won't be alone. Fear, the "not enoughs," and doubt will be there with you…reminding you of your past and attempting to shift your focus to what you may lack. But I am equally confident that if you step into that moment and embrace all the possibilities present, you will be meeting destiny.

It's your moment of decision. Will you take it? Or, will you spend another day with things staying the same? I vote that you cut the CRAP and step into your moment. The life you've been waiting for will meet you there.

Transformation comes with action, so here are some practical things you can do to cut the C-R-A-P:

The best way to handle the cynic is to limit your interactions and to address their negativity. You have to know when you can and can't handle the exposure. In my own life, I find the best antidote to a cynic is optimism. I protect my spirit with an intentional focus on the positive. I make sure to end every conversation or thought positively. In most circumstances, people will become trained to expect you to see the bright side. Positivity can make you unattractive to the cynic.

If you're struggling with regrets from the past, here are some, "activation steps", you can take:

1. **Learn From It:** All education costs something. Our mistakes can be the greatest lessons in life if we choose to learn from them. We have to be intentional about getting past the emotions and moving into the power of the experiences by reframing them. I make mistakes, but I don't let them change me into anything without my consent.

    Activate It! Today, make a list of your top five regrets. Then, ask yourself who you would be if you didn't have those experiences. Oftentimes, you will find that you were made better after making those choices.

2. **Lead From It:** Often, the power of our regret is that we haven't taken the time to invest it in others. The power of a story is that it gets told. Too often, we are ashamed of our failures, but the truth is that we are not alone. If we dare to share it with others, we empower others to learn valuable lessons.

    Activate It! After identifying how you grew as a result of your mistakes, work to understand how you can help others by the lessons you've learned. Be intentional about connecting and sharing with others to determine the types of people who will most benefit from your experience. Research and plan ways you can connect with them and begin executing.

3. **Leave It:** Sometimes, we can't make it right, despite out best efforts. Forgive yourself!

Intention is the antidote for apathy – spend at least five minutes each night examining your emotions, and when little things bother you throughout the day, investigate the reasons.

Practice self-awareness. Own your feelings, opinions, and thoughts. Spend time becoming more familiar with what it is you really want. When in a crowd, don't just say what you think everyone wants to hear. Take the time to listen to and honor your voice.

Coach Felicia

Ring the Alarm
Arise Into Your Purpose

Have you ever been in a place so low and full of despair that you had no idea how you would get out of such a cold, dark place? Have you spent sleepless nights with "bowed head and lowered eyes, shoulders falling down like teardrops, weakened by soulful cries"? When Maya Angelou wrote those words, I couldn't help but think of how she knew. How could she have known what it felt like to be broken and battered, looked down upon and ridiculed because of your greatness? I came to the conclusion that she knew because she lived it. She experienced indescribable pain from the terrors of her life. She learned her purpose through her trials. Maya Angelou wanted to teach us to "rise up from a past that's rooted in pain" to shine bright like the "diamonds at the meeting of [our] thighs." Ring the alarm and rise.

A journey doesn't end with the pain. It begins with it. So know that these tests are only the beginning of something so new and so refreshing that the only way to understand its greatness is to live through its vice.

Let's take a journey through the life of a woman I mentored from New York City who inspired me to start my *#BeingEmpoweredStilettos* campaign. At thirty-five years old, Faith had it all together. She was a mother, teacher, and entrepreneur with dreams to make it big in the fashion industry. Although she had the drive and passion needed for the fashion world, she didn't have the confidence to make her dreams a reality, so she sat on them. She focused on her daughter and men because that was where she found comfort. She knew the importance of having a strong male figure in her daughter's life who would love her like she was his own. For her, dating was easy but she had a list of prerequisites that a man had to meet in order to take things further. Although she hadn't taken time to become like the partner she was seeking, she knew who and what she wanted. She finally met the man she believed was her match. Despite not meeting her requirements of having a master's degree and six-figure salary, she decided to give him a chance. He wasn't as educated as she was but he had a job, attended church, loved his mother, and was definitely easy on the eyes. She gave her all to him and within seven months, they had become serious. They did everything together just as she wanted and her focus began to lean more towards pleasing him than pleasing herself and her daughter. After a year, he had convinced her to move miles away from her family and they moved in together. She changed jobs to earn more money and invested her savings into a condominium even though it was out of her price range. Things were going well until he lost his job and with it went his manhood. He had lost himself and began misdirecting his anger toward her. He was verbally and emotionally abusive but because he hadn't physically hit her, she stayed and tried to work it out, like many others would. His abuse and overcompensation for what he lacked caused her to lose herself and her worth. She didn't feel beautiful anymore because she had always relied on others to give her purpose. Because he was out of work, their roles began to shift and became one-sided. She paid the bills, managed the home, and carried her load as well as his. As her resentment began to build, the level of mutual respect in their relationship dwindled and all balance was lost. Issues they had overcome in the past began to resurface with a vengeance and a door for the enemy had opened. Soon after year three had passed, she lost her job, their home, and became pregnant. His inability to cope with the crumbling of what he desired to be his empire caused him to leave. She was forced to live in a shelter and become a single parent for the second time. With two small children and no hope, Faith was at her wits' end. It was time for her to ring the alarm. She was at that place that Maya Angelou encourages us to start from.

Start from the bottom and rise.

The *#BeingEmpoweredStilettos* campaign started for women like Faith with similar stories. We watch scripted reality TV shows, idolize fictional characters like Mary Jane, and engulf ourselves so much in others' realities that we believe it makes our problems less relevant. We mask our pain and hide behind fake smiles. We don't realize how these facades sculpt our characters with fantasy belief principals that are unrealistic and clouded. I challenge you to become who you were purposed to be in spite of what society depicts. I once heard a metaphor that resonated so much with me that I will never forget it:

The president mandated everyone with problems and painful stories to bag them up and bring them all to the capitol. The people with the most pain would be compensated for their troubles. So you bag up your story. Big black garbage bags full of abuse, depression, self-hate, poverty and obesity. As you walk towards the capitol, you can see people with bags twice the size of yours. You see children carrying their bags and their parents' bags and you begin to reflect. You then turn to your left and see your close friends carrying bags you never even knew they had. You turn around with your bags in hand and go back home.

While you are bitter and busy complaining about what you are going through, someone is dying. While you are angry and annoyed at what he or she has done to you, someone has lost their children in a custody battle. While you are frustrated that things didn't work out as planned, a mother is rummaging through garbage cans to feed her children. Take heed of the problems you have and find a solution for them rather than wallow in sadness.

> *"Do not free a camel of its hump; you may be freeing him from being a camel."*
>
> -Gilbert K. Chesterton

Our burdens come in many shapes and sizes and in varying levels of intensity, but they shape who we are in the present. They are our reference points for how we react to experiences we face. There are three sources of the pain we encounter. The first source of pain is self-inflicted. Very often we make choices that leave us in predicaments we cannot get out of easily, such as choosing to date an unavailable man. You make a choice to live in the moment of temporary gratification. Your child doesn't respect you because you chose to raise him or her the way you have by blaming your decisions on the absence of the father. Your job is in jeopardy because you chose to call in sick to go on vacation. You must live with your choices.

The second source of pain is inflicted by the enemy. Whether through using other people or our own elements of weakness, the devil unleashes his wrath in an attempt to conquer his greatest enemy. Addiction is a prime example of how the enemy can swoop in and pick at every weakness you have not yet conquered. The devil will even use your friends to gossip about you and feed your mind with lies that hinder your growth.

The third source of our pain is allowed by God. Yes, we serve a loving God but He knows that in order for us to experience and understand the greatness of good, we need to know bad when we see it. We need to know pain to bask in the glory of joy. Understand that in these instances, God will never give you pain that you cannot bear and every test you face is done in order to give you more material for your testimony. Learn the lesson so your hurt isn't in vain.

Then there are those people who give the "but factors"…

"…But getting ill was not my fault. I didn't choose to be sick. I didn't ask for my mother to pass away and I didn't decide to get raped. Why would I choose for my child to be autistic?"

Live a new lesson.

Life is a result of cause and effect. As a spiritual person, I believe that everything happens for a reason and more than likely, some choices you made resulted in a situation you are currently facing. And if you did not make a choice to get into the situation, for that predicament, the choice must come afterward.

Often you will experience the "why" before the "what" and you must choose the outcome of your pain. There is a spiritual law of attraction. Understand that your spiritual energy will not attract anything you cannot withstand. Your spirit may have attracted that adulterous man so you can learn to respect yourself in order for him and others to know your worth. Your spirit attracted that sickness for you to choose to live. You have a choice either before or after the issue arises.

A defeatist attitude will only keep you in a defeated world surrounded by dry, suffocating air. It will keep you standing on a broken foundation with a bleeding heart, hardened by the pain you are choosing to hold on to.

Choose a new beginning.

Face the results of poor decisions and choose victory going forward. You don't have to keep the rape a secret; it could mean someone else's healing. You don't have to allow your teenager to walk away; you could work on filling the void. You don't have to watch your business fail; you could choose to get a coach.

If you are not where you want to be, it's because you are choosing to live with unclear goals. You are choosing to stay stuck because if you truly had a burning desire to live anew, you would ring the alarm and make it happen.

Take the road less traveled.

Get crystal clear on the burning desires you have for happiness and choose to live.
People often tell you to stand up and move on, to let the past go and live. What they fail to tell you is how to do this. *How am I going to get out of this hole that I've created to become anything more than what I currently stare at in this dirty mirror?* I suggest you clean the mirror and take these five **"*activation steps*"** to rise and shine into your purpose:

1. **Wake Up with Intent**

    As you roll over and just before you get out of the bed, name the things you are thankful for. Name the things that you have forgiven yourself and others for. Affirm that today is going to be an extraordinary day and go for it.

2. ***Seek First to Understand More Than Being Understood***

   Take a step back and put yourself in the shoes of others. Perspective is everything, so understand that you may present yourself in a way that renders the results you are receiving. Take time to live a love philosophy and lead a logically loving life. Become who you want to attract into your circle.

3. ***Knowledge is Power***

   Make a commitment to yourself to read regularly. The book you missed won't help you. You can't receive the lesson or gain the knowledge if you haven't read the book, so feed yourself uplifting and inspiring knowledge that will aid you in finding your purpose.

4. ***Turn Up***

   Have fun. At least once a week, do something by yourself, for yourself. If you enjoy going to the movies like I do, go see a movie alone. Go take a class or work out. Take time out of your busy-ness to enjoy life the way you see fit.

5. ***Write the vision and make it plain***

   Write everything down. Start a journal. Write to-do-lists. Jot down ideas. De-clutter your mind by releasing your mess onto paper. Your mind is for building your dreams; don't keep it cluttered with things you can't change or ideas you haven't pursued. Writing will give clarity to your thoughts and release stress from your mind.

I am who and where I am today because I took these action steps very seriously. Procrastination and a need to fill voids caused during my childhood were the weaknesses the enemy saw in me and used to keep me complacent and empty. Before my son, I was content with teaching and collecting my check every other week. It was what I saw everyone else doing so it became my comfort zone. However, there was more in store for me. I birthed a king, met my mentor John W. Carter, found my passion, and doors I never knew existed began opening. My goals began to surface as each day I sought clarity and found it. I developed a burning desire to live my purpose of empowering and inspiring. In the very order I have advised you to take these steps; I too took them and have seen firsthand the results of rising above. I have seen firsthand what the late and great Maya Angelou saw so many years ago. Because I rang the alarm and activated my passion and purpose, I can now be that "rainbow in someone else's cloud."

I remember growing up during the times when everyone loved sunflower seeds. When they came out with the different flavors, it was heaven. We would spend our last quarter to buy a pack only to chew them up, suck the life out of them, and spit them out. We didn't realize that although edible, sunflower seeds are not meant to be sucked on and spit out. They are meant to be planted. What we didn't know growing up is that those seeds were truly symbolic of relationships. Every encounter we have with people we come across can develop into a relationship. Depending on how good of a gardener you are, the relationship will either live or die. In order to rise and shine into your purpose, the first relationship we must foster is with the Light. God is the Sun and we provide the water for our relationship with Him. Sometimes we get so caught up watering other seeds or sucking them dry, we forget to water the most important relationship in our garden.

Your seed with God gives life to all the other relationships, not vice versa. When your garden is well-cared for, you can reap the benefits the Sun has allowed to blossom. You can wake up each morning and plant more seeds. You can build more relationships that will help your garden grow so you can leave a legacy for those who will come after you. By caring for my garden and rising into my purpose, I have developed a circle of like-minded activators. I can show my son who he was purposed to be before society can tell him who he is. As more troubles and issues come (because trust and believe me when I say they don't stop), I am now equipped to handle them with style and grace. I can rise and shine each day because I am an overcomer. I am an Empowered Stilettos woman with balance and vision, stepping out each day to fulfill my purpose.

Stephanie Fleary

Don't Stop 'til You Get Enough
Recovering A Sense of Confidence and Authenticity

I am very committed and extremely passionate about what I do. I have gone through my share of struggles which had me feeling broken and defeated, but through perseverance and wanting to rebuild myself, I experienced my very own rebirth. While I do not consider myself to be the most outgoing person or the life of any party, I know God has imparted something unique and special within me, which enables me to sympathize yet not become a crutch and to empathize yet still know when to let go. For years, I have prayed asking God, "What is my purpose?" only to find that I was already standing in it, but had neglected to live it. If at any time I was asked of my convictions, I would declare that I based all things upon my faith. Until I was educated by life that "Faith is not determined by what we say; instead, it's realized by what we do."

On my journey to building the confidence I wanted but didn't have, I fought emotional highs and lows on a continual basis. There were days where I felt as though living was the last thing I wanted to do because it was taking more work and commitment from me than I was truthfully willing to give. Just simply smiling in sincerity was painstakingly hard to do. What was the purpose of my existence? Why was I needed? Who would even miss my presence? These questions came from my warped reasoning and thinking. I learned how to become an actress in my own life. I was always in character just in case others were watching. Needless to say, living a lie was the only way I knew how to live. My vision didn't allow me access to seeing a future that was filled with prosperity and happiness, especially since I was told nothing good would ever be mine. My headspace was corrupted by many negative messages that were planted into me, and due to my naiveté I believed everything that was uttered. What reasons were there for me to question the validity of what was said to or about me? I had absolutely no worth. Had God created me to suffer in a life of anguish? What had I done that this should be my reward?

Useless and hopeless are the words I use to describe the person I was, the person I was shaped into. None of us are born to think that way; just like everything else in life, it's a learned behavior, which we were taught, and since I was not strong enough, there was no way for me to fight this battle that was waging a war within me. I had to adjust my mindset, for if I didn't, I was surely doomed. Many saw how I was always eager to help. They would also offer compliments about how well I handled life as they claimed to notice how I allowed nothing to break me. The funny thing is they became extras in the production of my life without even knowing I was feeding off of what they thought I was so they wouldn't find out the truth of who I really was. I kept the anger and hurt built up inside for years, until eventually it became my protective covering.

If I ever slipped with the beliefs that people were trustworthy, then I had my anger to remind myself that everyone was the same, with one motive and impure intentions. It gave me the excuse I needed to not care about myself, to not love myself, to see myself as not being deserving of even the air that so many took for granted. This self-loathing coupled with negative distortions carried over into my adult years and followed me into my marriage. My husband didn't even know the real person he was married to because even with him, I was still the leading actress who made certain, he wouldn't be able to figure it out. It wasn't a role I loved playing; however, it's one that I felt compelled to do in order to keep judgments from being hurled in my direction yet again. For every difficult path I crossed I blamed life, deeming it the culprit which placed every hurtful stigma upon my back. There were so many times I remembered crying out to God asking, "Why was I the one chosen to suffer in this way?" "What type of punishment is this that You have bestowed upon me?" "Have I done wrong in a past life and these are the ramifications for my actions of which I had no keen knowledge?" For every day my eyes were opened, I hated life even more.

While I disliked living, there was one thing that still led the pack of every bitterness I had inside; it was the face I was forced to look at daily and there was no way to avoid that encounter because the face was my reflection. I knew how to smile with everyone else, I knew how to support everyone else, I even knew how to love everyone else, yet that reflection I saw daily I felt no connections to. In my heart I wanted to heal, but then there was that other part of me which thought I was getting exactly what was due me. My soul was damaged, filled with darkness, and afraid of the light, for only God knows what else would have been seen by others and I had to keep up this charade. It was a game I played and played very well. Here's my confession: I knew I wanted to have children so I could give the love to them that I felt I was never given, but the main reason I wanted children was because I knew I would be in control of who they loved. Therefore, they would love me, they wouldn't see my flaws, and they would only know me as "Mommy" and love me as such. It was perfect planning.

My husband told me he loved me, but how was I to be sure that he meant it; especially since I was told nobody would or could ever love me? Due to what I was told, I perceived his testament of love was a well-structured building compiled of dishonesty, as he was saying what he had to in order to receive what he wanted. My thinking was seriously flawed considering how much I truly thought everything in life was a sentencing of punishments. During my pregnancies I felt as though my womb had become one of my very curses, due to the awful experiences I went through which ripped away more pieces of me, pieces I no longer owned. My children though would be my creation; therefore, it was a situation I could control, and their love would definitely be mine. Four children were my gifts to myself, because they only saw the person who would love and nurture them and they had to give back their hearts and love to me. My imperfections were thrown heavy blows towards my face when I had my daughter; her birth became my revelation that I was completely damaged, dysfunctional in thoughts, and was thoroughly incapable of teaching her how to be a confident woman. How was I to teach what I was not equipped with? How was I to help her in her transition from child to adult, when the skills required were not at my disposal? Each time she looked in my eyes smiling, I felt the hardened exterior of my heart soften more. I had to fix myself for her sake. She was my motivator for change as nothing else gave me a reason to want better for myself—neither my husband nor our three boys whom God had so graciously blessed us with had this role in helping me fix myself.

In that moment, all things became clear. My children were not my gifts to myself; rather, they were my gifts given from God, because my daughter was my healing, my breakthrough, my deliverance from the loathing I embraced for years. I learned that what I saw as my curse was actually my blessing. The problem was that I wasn't properly positioned to receive any of it. My daughter helped me change the outlook I had on myself. My outlook helped me to improve my confidence, and my confidence helped me to empower others. I saw that there was so much more to me and all I needed to do was to create positive daily affirmations to feed my soul. I saw through the eyes of my daughter how valuable I was as a woman, and all my children taught me how much love I had to give, while my husband taught me how much I deserved in return.

My **shackles of insecurities** were about to be broken, and my **vows** I took to **confidence were about to reveal all of life's misinterpretations I believed, based on what I previously heard and entertained.** Once I took responsibility for my growth and the things that I allowed to take root, I was able to repair what needed repairing. In the past, I professed having tons of faith, but where was that faith I spoke so highly of, the faith I eagerly sold to others who walked around with their own broken esteem and distortions? I was a fraud to their lives, but an even bigger fraud to the person that needed me the most: **ME**. I talked the talk, but I didn't walk the walk. When I recognized the truth of the situation, I didn't pity myself; I made the step to change the ways I spoke when behind closed doors because my negative words were keeping me a prisoner in my own world, a world that was built by others for me. The worst part was that when I got older and I saw that it was not a suitable way for me to live; I fed myself all the negative reasons as to why it was acceptable. I made the ultimate decision to pull myself out of the rut which I had lived in for years. I stopped allowing people to give their unsolicited opinions of who they thought I was or should be. It was time for me to become **empowered** so I could stand in my greatness, elevating myself to firmly plant my feet on the platform God carved out for me. I experienced my **rebirth** when I released the cobwebs of negativity from my head space, and it began my journey of healing which was long overdue.

The process forced me to re-vamp my very appearance, I changed the way I walked, talked, but more importantly, I learned to love myself. It no longer mattered if I wasn't as thin as others said I should be. It no longer concerned me whether people thought of me as beautiful or not. When I smile now, I do it freely and with total honesty. Now I have a confidence that only God alone has the ability to diminish if He so chooses. Through the improving of self, I was finally able to really help others on their journeys of **soul empowerment with self-improvement**. I came to understand that it was my own lack of faith and belief in myself that kept me from reaching my full potential. Too many times we give away the authority of ourselves to others, which doesn't make sense on any level no matter which way we look at it. We become so caught up with what everyone else is saying, doing, and what they look like we never stop for one minute to ponder the thoughts of what they might be feeling.

I was one of those very people. My fixation on others did nothing for improving my self-worth. It served to heighten theirs while I became my personal assailant hindering myself from excelling. What good could I be to my children if I couldn't stand being in my own presence? I made everything a distraction just so I could have an excuse as to why I couldn't do what needed to be done. While I was self-sabotaging, I failed to realize that it wasn't only about me; I was also sabotaging my children's futures. We have to pay close attention to even the tiniest details because those are the things that can make the biggest impact, whether bad or good. Due to self-negligence, I affected one of my children and he is now a mirror image of who I was. I can't blame him for that, but I am now forced to take responsibility for what I have done to him. I thought they weren't watching but they saw everything. I thought they weren't listening, but he heard it all. Now his lack of confidence is my backlash for refusing to rise up from the ashes of insecurities. It's my pain that I am faced with daily, my hurt that I must repair before he becomes a man. This is our wake-up call: people only focus on destroying wholesome and strong things which pose a threat, because they do not see the greatness in us because we have trained ourselves not to see. Every circumstance in life presents a lesson to be learned. The question is how open are we to embrace and learn what is being taught?

Not every lesson is going to be given by an educator, doctor, pastor or instructor. Many will be given by life itself. We all come from different walks, and with those walks we have developed our own stories and it is those stories that we must use as a tool of empowerment. Fixing up the outside with makeup, name brands, fast cars and caviar cannot fix what requires repair. What are you going to do when you are left sitting in a room with just your reflection and your thoughts? How can we help others, when we are more damaged than those we are trying to impress? What good are you to your children if you can't even stand to look at yourself? Before we can say we love and value others, we must first be able to love and value ourselves, because we are our first love. I bear the scars and hurts of what I have done to myself. It is something that I have got to face every day of my life because I was too chicken to take a stand and fight for my own happiness. Life never told me that I was to be unhappy. Life never told me I was not good enough. Life never told me I deserved to suffer. What it did show was that I needed to do right by me and stop allowing others to validate me.

Confidence is about standing in "your greatness" without desiring or needing approval from others. Confidence is about knowing your voice is mightier than any spoken words of another. Confidence is acknowledging that you are a person of phenomenal attributes whose validations come from within. Confidence is believing that you are wonderfully made, for there is none other like you. Confidence is knowing that you are ENOUGH!

When it comes to self-confidence, there is an undeniable difference between one who exhibits feelings of tenacity and one who is afraid of his or her own shadow. Sometimes we have to force ourselves to emote what we are feeling in order to get to the place where we need to be. Confidence and faith are like a picture revealing one's mental state, which is no different from any other emotion one is privy to. It will either be displayed as a masterpiece or a piece missing from its master. Emotions consisting of strong definitive urges, completeness, regality, and assuredness are what you need to possess instead of acting as if they are a part of a role you are given to play.

Let confidence and faith be readily noticeable in your actions and speech. It is something that only we alone are able to promote for ourselves, yet it can be taken away by the mere insolence of others. An enduring confidence cannot be swayed, for its strength is not of such that can be defeated by the tyrannical operations of naysayers. Allow confidence to be the crutch of what you shall lean upon and allow it to be your voice of empowerment, neglecting the sting of death invited by the mouths of others.

Confidence is a **priceless gift**, which others can help to cultivate, but we alone are able to provide it with nourishment for **prosperous growth**. Confidence is the foundation on which dreams are built and a power tool can cause destruction to the manifestation of visions coming into fruition. If there is refusal of utilizing it to its full capacity, then the soul shall **perish**.

Activation Steps to Confidence

1. Cease all "stinking thinking"... it only leads to negative compensation.
2. Cease self-doubts... this is the mindset of one who has programmed him or herself to accept complacency as the highest level of achievement.
3. Cease self-criticism by implementing positive affirmations. Embrace who you are, not who you were told to be.
4. Be intentional with your living, leaving nothing to chance.

Ophelia Uke

Contributors

Vasavi Kumar

Vasavi Kumar is often described as "your kick-in-the-pants guide en route to your desired destination." An entrepreneur at heart, Vasavi holds dual Master's degrees in Special Education from Hofstra University and Social Work from Columbia University. She's co-author of the bestselling book *Succeeding in Spite of Everything*, has been featured in *The Wall Street Journal*, and was a regular on NBC as the "Keepin' It Real" guru on *Kansas City Live*, as well as a featured Life Coach on VH1's *Basketball Wives* where she coached one of the main stars of the show. In 2013, after setting her "nourish the minds of the people" goal in place, Vasavi set out to complete her purpose's equation to "nourish the mouths of the people." Vasavi pursued her dream of becoming a vegetarian chef at The Natural Epicurean Academy of Culinary Arts in Austin, Texas. She has committed to dedicating her life to show people how to nourish themselves by being conscious about what they eat, how they think, and what they do, in order to serve "bigger" in the world. See more of Vasavi at www.vasavikumar.com

Coach Felicia

Her passion inspires, her honesty connects and her practical wisdom transforms the lives of women—and men—ready to maximize their potential—in every area of life. In the words of bestselling author Lisa Nichols, Coach Felicia is an "instant girlfriend" whose "message crosses gender, socio-economic, cultural and religious lines because it is that of the human spirit." Coach Felicia's compelling, personal and professional narrative has engaged audiences and clients such as General Electric,

Time Inc., eWomenNetwork, Proctor & Gamble, Ketchum, National Association of Black MBAs, National Association of Black Journalists, Kaplan, Pearson Education and Fordham University. Coach Felicia holds a BA in Sociology from New York University and a M.Ed. in Adult & Organizational Learning from Northeastern University. She lives by the credo "Once you discover your worth, you will experience true wealth. Do your work and watch your dreams move towards you!" See more of Felicia at www.coachfelicia.com

Stephanie Fleary

Empowerment facilitator, author and event producer is a force to be reckoned with in the personal development industry. As an educator for almost ten years she has counseled broken mothers, helpless children and dwindling families; aiding in the repair and need for growth.

As a result of the knowledge and experience she has gained as well as her love for shoes, Ms. Fleary founded Empowered Stilettos LLC in 2013 to teach confidence and balance to women from all walks of life. A personal development company specializing in producing empowerment events, Empowered Stilettos has developed and implemented workshops for educators of the Diocese of Brooklyn in addition to collaborating with The Institute 4 Increased Performance working diligently to introduce "The Making of a Champion" series to those in search of more. Not only does this stiletto queen have the keen ability to bring people together for a cause but she is also able to call them into action. See more of Stephanie at about.me/Stephanie.Fleary

Ophelia Uke

Ophelia Uke is a talented writer who had to overcome many obstacles on her journey of success. Her West Indian background was one of a strict upbringing, wherein God and education was at the forefront. She graduated from Harry S. Truman high school in NY. Shortly after, she moved to Connecticut to attend College. Nursing was her career major. Years later she married, moved, gave up working, and became a full time mom. Growing up, she was referred to as a loner, not desiring the need of a lot of friends. However, she desperately desired acceptance. Vocalizing her feelings was not something she did.

Ophelia became a writer, because she finally found her voice, and through her words, she saw how she was able to inspire others. Now, her mission is helping others release their insecurities and/or pains, whether it is from the past or in the present, so they can move forward building a happier and better future as she has found, and is living today. See more of Ophelia at www.opheliauke.com

LIVE RICHER™

One of the biggest things I had to release before moving forward was "external thinking." For so long I did what I was told or expected to do and lived how I thought I ought to live. I never stopped to really choose what I wanted, needed, desired. I thought externally, versus internally. From time to time, I would look outside myself for the answer and as a result, always felt like something was missing. Once I let go of "external thinking," everything changed.

I sought motivation *within* first. I began to talk to God more and actually started listening. I learned to be still and let myself be guided by my "higher self." As I tapped into the God within, my support system sought me out. The closer I got to living my purpose, the more I attracted people who wanted to assist me on my journey.

My Core Message of Activation

LIVE RICHER™! Live a life that is purposeful and passionate! Be strong, generous, loving, and kind. At the age of 29, I quit my old life and started a new one. I activated my core message by taking a leap of faith and started my own business, The Budgetnista.

Activation Steps

1. You want a dream life—start now! There is no better time than the present.
2. Do away with self-doubt, negative inner chatter and comparing self to others. Keeping it will only hinder you from living richer.
3. Stay away from chasing after social success.
4. Stop making excuses! Your purpose and destiny are much larger than your excuses.

This next set of stories further shares how you can "LIVE RICHER™!"

Tiffany "The Budgetnista" Aliche

Smooth Operator
Using The Power of Forgiveness

> "God often uses our deepest pain as the
> launching pad of our greatest calling."
> -Author Unknown

I'll never forget the day that I received the unwanted telephone call. It was January 19, 2011 at 9:57 a.m. I remember it as if it was yesterday. My doctor called to tell me that I had breast cancer. My personal life was already in despair. It had been four months since I had walked away from my fifteen-year marriage, and surely I didn't need this bad news. So many emotions were going through my mind; hurt, despair, betrayal, resentment, and unforgiveness. I was not in a good place emotionally, mentally, or spiritually. My immediate family had been ripped apart and there were people who were being used by the devil to try to destroy me and my character. The devil comes to steal, kill, and destroy, and he wasn't holding back any punches.

I couldn't fight my enemies in the physical sense because I now had to fight for my life. Where did this thing called breast cancer come from? No one in my immediate family had it, so how did I get it? Was I going to die from it? I had to learn that the Bible said that "this sickness is not unto death." Breast cancer was everything I needed, which I will explain later, but nothing I ever wanted. God had to keep me from myself because there were times that I thought that I was going to lose my mind. There was this "new" feeling that I was having; it snuck up on me, it was starting to overtake me, and it was the spirit of unforgiveness. How did I get to this point in my life? Sure, people have treated me wrongly before, but I was experiencing pain at a new level in my life now, and I was spinning out of control.

I had to find comfort and peace in dealing with forgiveness, and it was an awkward feeling. I like other words that begin with the letter "F," like faith, family, football, food, and fun… but people cringe when you start talking about forgiveness. I thought about particular scriptures such as Matthew 6:12 & 14-15 KJV: "And forgive us our debts, as we forgive our debtors… For if ye forgive men their trespasses, your heavenly Father will also forgive you; but if ye forgive not men their trespasses, neither will your Father forgive your trespasses."

So, God, you're telling me that I have to forgive people who have lied on me, talked badly about me, tried to discredit my character, broken up my family, put me in financial ruins, and abused me emotionally and verbally? Really, God, You can't be serious! I talk to God like I talk to a regular person, and I would say, "God, you know darn well that what they are doing and saying isn't right, and yet You want me to forgive them?" or, "God, I don't know how much longer I can do this "forgiveness thing" or, "God, I don't want to fall prey to these violent emotions and end up regretting the outcome," or, "God, how can people who say they love You purposely hurt me with their actions and their words? And you want me to turn the other cheek?" There were times when I didn't want to obey God because I felt that He wasn't moving fast enough to "get them back." I didn't want to love those who hurt me, I didn't want to pray for them, and I just wanted to lash out. But God kept convicting me with His Word. You know how you keep telling your children to do something and they know that it's for their own good but they don't want to do it? That's how God was dealing with me and my spirit of unforgiveness. I kept coming across scriptures in the Bible that were "stepping on my toes." For example, Matthew 5:44 KJV says, "But I say unto you, love your enemies; bless them that curse you, do good to them that hate you, and pray for them which despitefully use you, and persecute you." *Whew! Now, God, You are asking a bit much! Now you want me to pray for my enemies? You want me to do good to folk when I know they are stabbing me in the back?* When I began to be obedient to the Word, I started calling out the names of my enemies in prayer, asking God to watch over them and to protect them and their families. I would ask God to soften their hearts so that they too can be whole. At first I wondered, "Did I just call out that person's name?" But soon, this became a daily part of my prayer life. When I started actively applying the principles of forgiveness in my life, divine connections started happening, unspeakable blessings came pouring down, and I found myself in a place of peace.

I've had people say to me, "Wanda, I don't know how you went through all that you did: a divorce and battling breast cancer at the same time and yet you forgave those people. Girl, if it were me, I honestly don't know if I could do it." I couldn't harbor any resentment or bitterness, because at the end of the day, I had to take ownership of the fact that I allowed myself to be treated with disrespect. I allowed myself to be in wrong situations. I didn't know the power of the word "No." I didn't know my own self-worth, so I settled for relationships that weren't ordained by God. Nelson Mandela made a profound statement in his quote, "As I walked out the door toward the gate that would lead to my freedom, I knew if I didn't leave my bitterness and hatred behind,

I'd still be in prison." I was not in a physical prison, but I was in an emotional, mental, and spiritual prison, and forgiveness was my key to escaping. In the Bible, David said that it was good that he had been afflicted. Likewise, breast cancer saved my life because it taught me how to forgive. I couldn't have had one or the other; I needed breast cancer and forgiveness to work hand-in-hand in my life. This was my road to Damascus and there were some major potholes on this road to forgiveness, but I couldn't fall to pieces, and I couldn't break down every time the enemy tried to throw something my way. My main pothole was a lack of forgiveness. This was a bad feeling that had entered into my spirit and I knew that it was wrong. God had to place a sign on me that said "Under Construction." During this molding process, the new pothole was filled with forgiveness, love, peace, compassion, and filled with a top coat of favor!

God can use your problem not only as a testimony, but to usher you into your promise. I needed all of my low moments so that God could mold, restore, and humble me. I'm grateful that God trusted me with the spirit of forgiveness, which in turn forced me to have an intimate relationship with Him. I now use forgiveness as a platform for others to seek Him. Is forgiveness easy? No! Forgiveness sounds like an easy process, but it isn't! It's a daily and sometimes hourly journey. Women, we know that forgiveness is not easy for us. We are emotional creatures; we want to react when we feel like we've been hurt and betrayed. The one who was offended needs to forgive first—not for the betterment of the other person, but for his or her own sake. Not only forgive the other person(s) involved for their actions, but forgive yourself as well. *Now, that sounds hard—how do I forgive myself?* You may wonder. Well, you have to forgive yourself for allowing the hurt to hurt you. You know the saying "Hurt people, hurt people."? You have to realize that people come into your life for a season, reason or lifetime. What lesson did you learn? You can either be bitter or be better. Why not choose the latter?

My darkest moments defined my life. They taught me who was there for me. Everybody can say that they support you until it's time to actually support you. Those moments taught me that I had to rely on God and my faith started to increase. My once troubled spirit became quiet and I was able to hear the voice of God. Family ties grew stronger and forgiveness became easier. I believe that it's not what a life-threatening disease takes from you that counts—what counts is what you do with what you have left. I kept propping myself up on people and being so dependent on them that God took away my crutches and forced me to trust in Him. When the enemy threw me in the fire, he had no idea that he was making me stronger. I knew in my spirit that when I came out of this fiery furnace, I was going to be stronger, I was going to be better, and I was going to be victorious. Isaiah 66:9 (NCV translation) says, "I will not cause pain without allowing something to new to be born,' says the Lord." I had to let my trials refine me; my purpose had to be birthed. I had to show others that I had to forgive, even when the flesh wanted me to seek revenge against those that wrongfully and spitefully used me. God said that he would never leave me nor forsake me, and through forgiveness, I found a peace that surpasses all understanding.

I wanted to feel peace for a long time, and realized that searching for it in toxic relationships and material things can take you to some very dark places. It's amazing what can happen when you give the wrong people control over your life. Telling others about forgiveness and how it healed me not only physically but also mentally and spiritually became my purpose in life; it became a ministry.

I have to think that the laughter and the tears go together. I'm always cracking jokes now because I'm free emotionally, mentally, and physically. The tears that I shed every morning when I put my hand over my left breast that was invaded by breast cancer aren't tears of sadness; they are tears of joy because I'm a survivor. Had it not been for the diagnosis, I wouldn't have had the strength to get my life together. Sometimes, opening up your eyes to situations can be the most painful thing to do. I do not define myself by how many disappointments I've faced. I define myself by the forgiveness and faith that I have found to begin again, and to forgive others. I do not define myself by how long my relationships lasted. I define myself by how much I have loved and how much I am willing to love again. I define myself by how many times I've fought to get back on my feet. I do not define myself by the physical scars that are left from my three breast cancer surgeries. I look at those scars as battle wounds, because I fought a tough battle and won. Yes, I've been dealt some low blows, but they didn't knock me down. They made me sway a little, but like Jay-Z said, I had to "get that dirt off my shoulder."

I've seen forgiveness take place in the most unconventional episodes and all of the sacrifices have been worth it. There's something so peaceful about using your scars (physical or emotional), your pain, your struggles, your heartaches, and your mistakes to help others. I feel so empowered when I speak to women about my journey with breast cancer survival and tell them about the power of forgiveness. It's therapeutic for me. I believe that through the pain, there was a plan. The cost of the oil in my alabaster box has been great, but I wouldn't change any part of my journey, because it all led me back to God. Sometimes our best lessons are learned through pain. Do people even realize the healing that comes through forgiveness? I believe that I had to pray for my enemies so that I could be healed (James 5:16). I didn't want my breast cancer to come back. I had to learn the power and freedom of forgiveness. I thought that if I forgave others, they would in turn forgive or apologize to me, and that hasn't happened. So, I have to be okay with an "I'm sorry" that I may never get. Forgiveness is a gift that you give to yourself. Forgiveness unblocks your blessings.

How to "Activate" Forgiveness

1. You can start by saying the Lord's Prayer below (Matthew 6:9-13 KJV). Trust and ask God to lead you through the Holy Spirit:

   After this manner therefore pray ye: Our Father which art in heaven, Hallowed be thy name. Thy kingdom come, Thy will be done in earth, as it is in heaven. Give us this day our daily bread. And forgive us our debts, as we forgive our debtors. And lead us not into temptation, but deliver us from evil: For thine is the kingdom, and the power, and the glory, forever. Amen.

2. You can have a "purging ceremony." Write a letter to yourself, detailing what you need to be forgiven for and who you need to forgive. Spare no thoughts. After you've done this, burn the letter and you will feel emotional freedom.

3. You may need to meet with the person(s) that you want to ask for forgiveness. Some people need that personal interaction to have closure.

4. You may never receive an "I'm sorry" from someone who has hurt you, and you have to walk in peace with that. It's not a reflection on you; it's a reflection on their lack of character. Pray for them and walk in strength. Have comfort that you've done your part and know it's up to God to work on their heart.

5. Toxic relationships can change your perception of what your reality really is. You may start thinking that you are worthless because of your past mistakes. Stay away from these negative thoughts and say daily affirmations to yourself. You can say "I am beautiful," "I am whole," "I am forgiven," "I am a conqueror," "I am worthy," and "I am loved." The Bible says in Proverbs 27:7 KJV "As he thinketh in his heart, so is he." Don't just say these words; act on your belief.

God gave me beauty for ashes. Forgiveness gave me strength, victory, and healing. I am not my past; I am that which has emerged from the fire. I am a woman that has finally found calmness within herself through forgiveness, because I now walk in peace – not pieces. And you now have the tools to do the same.

Wanda Briscoe

Lovers Rock
The Journey to Self-Love

Self—*a person or thing referred to with respect to complete individuality.* (www.dictionary.com)

Love—*a profoundly tender, passionate affection for another person.* (www.dictionary.com)

I suspect that we all have come to a point in life where we questioned the love or felt the lack of love toward ourselves. The choice to love oneself ultimately determines how you will author your own life's story. As Harley-Davidson says, "When writing the story of your life, don't let anyone else hold the pen." Here is the story of my journey.

I've tried to take the easy way and not embrace things that challenged me to become my best self. I almost diminished the quality and real substance of who God created me to be because of my decision to live beneath my God-given ability, and trying to fit in with those I came into contact with. I always knew that I was going to be great, but was floating in the sea of being average, mediocre, people-pleasing, and harboring low self-esteem, self-sabotage, and doubt. Have you ever swum in those places? What I've learned is, we never accomplish as much when we only do the things that don't test us, stretch us, challenge us, or generally make us feel out of our "element." We are who we are because of the choices we make and the lack of self love in our lives.

The journey to loving self will take you out of your comfort zone. This means you have to work and dig constantly. This also means that, although the crossroads may be scary, making a difficult decision can cause you to see who you truly are and what you're made of. At the end of it all, you must realize that you were born for your assignment....you must trust the process. There are a lot of things that may be going through your mind. *I want to take the step; I don't want to take the step. I want to love my perfect imperfections; I don't want to love my flaws.* Personally, it was always a back-and-forth for me.

The Road to Loving Me

Let's go back in time for a moment. Starting in the early '80s, around the age of twelve, I can hear it now: my uncle hitting me on my head, saying, "Boy, don't you have a big head." Then I ran into the ladies' room and looked in the mirror to see how big my head really was. I looked forward and then I looked sideways, saying to myself, "there's nothing wrong with my head." But what happened was that I heard it so many times that those bathroom visits became frequent and dreadful. I would stay a little longer in the ladies' room, trying to push my head in, knocking it in to try to make it smaller, but realized that this was not good enough. So, before I would go to bed, I would use a head tie and ensure my head was covered really tightly, hoping that my head would shrink a bit. I prayed to God to please let my head be normal. Please let me have a small head.

Take a moment here to reflect. How many times have you done a re-evaluation of self based on what somebody else has said to you? I was almost a teenager and didn't realize that my head was "not normal." I then started to compare my head to others. I noticed that some heads were pointy, some were flat, some were bigger than mine, and ooh, I was so sorry for those ones. Comparison is a dangerous thing to do. This isn't to say that all comparison is bad, as sometimes we learn much from observing and adopting behaviors we'd rather pursue. But it's problematic the moment we label ourselves as somehow "not right" by comparison. I found out that I was not the only one who had flaws. No one's perfect and you just have to accept your flaws and learn to love yourself.

Thinking that was enough, it was time for me to begin high school. I encountered the same thing again. Looking at all the other girls in my class, I was one of the darker ones and noticed that my head was really big. I solved that problem by wearing bangs. I got by for a little while until one day, standing in the assembly line, a male classmate of mine shouted out, "Laquisha, you should stand in the middle of the line so that we can all balance." Everyone burst out into laughter. Guess who also laughed? Me. I laughed but I was hurting inside, wondering, *why me? Why do I have to look like this?* That same male said I had a forklift head and went on and on with big head jokes directed at me. I guess he thought he was Kevin Hart. I hated to go to class because I didn't know what the boys in my class were going to come up with next.

Things died down a bit as they started to torment someone else in the class. I thought, *yes! At least it's not me... at least not now...*but after a few weeks, the jokes turned back to me and continued throughout the school year. It was not only my head this time; it was also the fact that I was skinny and darker than most of my classmates. My name was changed from Laquisha to Olive, as in Popeye's wife from the cartoon, with the big head and skinny body. I remembered the school lights going out one day and boy, did the dark people in my class get it. The jokes continued, like, "who likes dark chocolate?" directed at me or other dark classmates. I was so happy to hear the school bell ring at 2:30 p.m. I was the first one out of the class and first one at the gate; that meant I could go home, to safety and a family who loved me.

I went through high school hating some things about my body that I eventually had to accept. One thing I've realized is that the journey to self-acceptance is one many people face at different stages in life, but the sooner you learn to embrace those perfect imperfections, the sooner you can stop letting them hold you back from making the necessary decisions for your awesome life journey.

Now that I've pinpointed my flaws as a teenager, it's time for you to do so also (if you don't have any, kudos to you). What flaws do you have? It doesn't have to be anything physical. Your flaw may be that you're a bad dancer. You're shy. You're an awful singer. You may talk too much.

Let's hear it: _____

Once it was time to go to college, I started to fully internalize society's current ideals of beauty and intelligence and felt like I didn't meet those ideals. As you can see, a flaw is very easily born. They may first be pointed out by family members, friends, or co-workers, but mainly come through another person's distorted image of desirable traits.

As I reflect on growing up, I realize my parents and siblings didn't mention my weight or the size of my head. Inside the home I was fine; the issues only came outside the safety of my home. But if you want to be great, you can't stay at home. You can't continue to hide. There's a real world out there and you have to face it. I've had, as I'm sure many other women have, defining points in life where something critical was said that stuck in my memory, like recalling all those times I was called Olive, forklift head, or dark chocolate. This unfortunately became a defining part of me in its own small, yet significantly unhelpful, way. Although I said during my adolescence years that "sticks and stones may break my bones, but words will never hurt me," I realized that although words did not physically hurt me, they did hurt internally. I was unhappy with the way God created me.

I always tried to make my parents smile, but based on some decisions I made, their smiles sometimes turned into frowns. My dad is a bishop and my mom a retired school teacher, so there was also the pressure to be and do things right. Because of who they were, growing up as a teenager, my siblings and I could not do things that our peers got to do. We faced a lot of pressure and expectations because of our last name and who our parents were. As a teenager, I didn't understand why our parents expected us to make certain grades, achieve at a certain level, or do a particular thing, but as time passed, I realized that their expectations were for our own benefit.

Now it was time to leave my parents and go to an unfamiliar land. Staying home and not furthering my education was not an option for me. My choice was to go to school, or to go to school. Yes, that's right; no choice. I decided to go off to college. Oh, the pressure of getting others to understand me. I felt as though I was not able to cross my *t*'s and dot my *i*'s. Here's where the true self-sabotage started. I thought because I had an accent, others wouldn't be able to understand what I was trying to articulate.

My living arrangements and my surroundings were new, and the people around me were new. I caught myself trying to sound like and emulate the people around me. Day by day I was losing myself as I tried to "fit in." I didn't want to be the odd one out. Coming from a place where everyone knew me, I couldn't do anything before it was reported back to my parents. Now, I just wanted people to think I was cool. I never mentioned what my parents did because society has this thing with "pastors' kids." I just wanted to be Laquisha and not a bishop's daughter. I embrace it now, but it took work. It took me accepting the family I was born in, the country that I was born in, and the accent that I had.

One day, my mom gave me the scripture found in Jeremiah 1:5, which is one of my favorites to this day. It reads, "Before I formed you, I knew you, I set you apart and you were called to the nations." (author's paraphrase) That was enough said. I carried that with me throughout my life.

Why try to fit in when we were born to stand out?

It took me a while to realize that what set me apart was not a burden, but what makes me great. Many women and men take too much energy and time trying to see how they can blend in. You don't ever want to be normal or average. Maya Angelou said it best: "When you know better, you do better." After all, why be normal when you can be exceptional? When something simply "fits in," it is too easy to blend in, to go completely unnoticed. But when something stands out, you cannot help but notice it, give your attention and be drawn to it. I am not talking about standing out in your physical appearance–I am talking about standing out with your character and being proud of where you came from. I am talking about being happy with the family you were born into. I am talking about going the extra mile, being kind and compassionate toward others, by living a life of integrity. Those qualities will definitely make you a person who stands out. Every day we have the choice to stand out and focus on being fabulous, to go beyond the average, to be exceptional. I can hear my parents saying it now: "Why follow the crowd when you can be leading it? Why shoot for ordinary when you can be spectacular?"

Although it had been a struggle for many years because the scenery was different and the people sounded different, I had to learn to be confident in the sound that was coming from my mouth. After all, I would not be me if I lost this part of my amazing self. It confused me when I heard people who came from where I came from sounding different from me. They totally lost their accent and who they were, but although I tried, I never lost mine, and now it made me stand out. Don't lower your standards to fit in with the crowd. Instead, let your example be what lifts others around you to raise their standards to yours. I assume if you're reading this chapter, you must be a leader, and if you are a leader, you lead by example. Don't worry about the crowd, but set your standards high.

What's in a name...?

I'm sure if I said the names Alejandro, Juan, Mary, Laquisha, Sheniqua, or London, you would be able to identify whether the person is Black, Caucasian, Hispanic or from some other place. You will have some assumptions about what you think a person does, what they have, the kind of environment they came from, and so on and so forth. But we can be wrong in so many ways when it comes to judging. I believe that no one should judge a book by its cover because the pages of the book are still being written. Who but God is to say what the outcome of your life will be, or when the last chapter of your life will be written?

When I introduced myself, people would sometimes say, "You've got a ghetto name." I also remembered a friend of my cousin saying to me, "what are you doing with that 'hood name?" They left me speechless. Society has contaminated us so much that just because a few people say something, everyone else judges by that negative assumption. Even in the life of reality TV, you will see a lot of the women either using a shorter version of their name or using a middle name because they are ashamed of their real name. Check it out for yourself. It seems as though no matter how high they get in life, they try to be something they're not. I was like those women on reality TV, too. I was thinking of ways to change my name so people would not look at me a certain way. A guy that was interested in me asked, "What's your *real* name?" I said "Laquisha *is* my real name." He went on to say that the only Laquishas he knew lived in the 'hood, with at least six kids, purple hair, and a whole lot of tattoos. I didn't know how to respond because he was really cute, but I was in shock. I was not familiar at all with the things that he named, but I just responded by saying I had none of the above and that he should not judge my name because it can be very offensive. Once, I went to a courthouse to see how I could legally change the name I had for all these years. I remembered asking my mother why she gave me that name. She was always there to give me direction. She said that just as I was made in love, my name was given to me in love. I've encountered other adults telling me once I introduced myself, "you don't look like a Laquisha." Hmmm, so now *Laquisha* has a "look."

Loving another more than self…

I remember dating my first love, someone I was head-over-heels for, who after four years cheated on me with someone lighter and smaller than me. I remember pleading with him to take me back, asking questions like, "is it because I'm dark, or is it my accent, or my weight?" He held me by both hands and said, "Just listen, do you hear how you sound?" He went on to say, "You deserve someone better." I was not willing to accept that and wanted to change my physical appearance so he would want me. Seeing so many commercials on cosmetic surgeries, I thought that surgery was an option. So I went for a consultation, got the date for my surgery, made my payment, and was ready to have a new body. All this, to get my boyfriend back! The date came for the surgery and I remember the doctor waking me up. I was still under sedation and going in and out. My friend who I trusted to take care of me after the surgery was there, too. The doctor said that the procedure could not be done because I needed to have medical clearance. Medical clearance? I was so upset because I was not going to be able to show my ex-boyfriend my "new body." I guess that was God's way of saying, no you won't do that. There are many people who are on missions to do things for others, on a mission for someone else's approval, validation, or love.

"Activating" Self Love

What I had to do was to say kind words about me, from me. If you're not doing this now, start today.

1. **Start talking positively to yourself.** Stop waiting for somebody to come by and tell you how fabulous you are. There was a time when I would've found it difficult to name three things I liked, let alone loved, about myself. Happily, today I have moved from that and am now able to share my story with others.

2. **Understand that self-love takes time.** It is a process and a journey. Self-love is made up of lots of little actions, repeated, like saying good things to yourself.

3. **"It doesn't matter where you came from, what your circumstances are, or what issues you have, your dreams are valid."** Lupita Nyong'o said it best at her acceptance speech at the Oscars. So I say to you, no matter how you look, no matter how you may sound, no matter what your name is, whatever others say about you, or how others feel about you, these things DO NOT MATTER! There's greatness within you that is lying dormant and needs to be activated.

4. **Embrace the fact you were not called to be mediocre; you were called to the nations.** You have a chapter that's yet to be written. You have to be proud of your story and not look at your shortcomings as disappointments but as life lessons.

5. **You must die to your old way of thinking**—things taught, thing said—in order to complete your journey.

My road of self-love has been an experience. Writing this brought back a lot of memories I just wanted to ignore and forget about. I had all these big dreams, but because I was not ready to accept who I was and all that came with me, I became stagnant. I was stuck at the crossroads of accepting myself. Stagnation is the enemy of progress, but sometimes it's easy to get caught up in all the things we want to change about ourselves and forget all about the wonderful things we already have going on. If this is an area you struggle with, I am sure it will be an experience for you as well. Congratulations on taking the first step to getting there.

Laquisha Williams

Contributors

Tiffany Aliche

Tiffany "The Budgetnista" Aliche is a speaker and passionate, award winning teacher of fun financial empowerment. Since 2008, The Budgetnista has specialized in the delivery of financial literacy education that includes seminars, workshops, curricula and trainings. Tiffany is also the bestselling author of the book, The One Week Budget (#1 Amazon / budgeting).

Tiffany is the financial literacy expert for City National Bank and she and her financial advice have been featured on the TODAY show, PBS, Pix11 Morning News, News 12 New Jersey, The New York Times, ESSENCE Magazine, FORBES, PBS, The Star Ledger, Ebony Magazine, Fox Business, MSNBC, Redbook, CBS Money Watch, Black Enterprise, USA TODAY, as well as numerous online publications. She also blogs about personal finance for The Huffington Post. See more of Tiffany and The Budgetnista at www.thebudgenista.com

LaQuisha Williams

LaQuisha Williams, Speaker, lifestyle Etiquette designer, Esteem Expert, mentor and founder of "Girl Connection" – a premier platform for progressive women designed to inspire personal development and social change and "The Purpose Circle" where women meet as strangers and become lifelong purpose partners. As a Lifestyle Etiquette Designer, she believes that every woman deserves to live a richer and fulfilling life without compromising her beliefs and morals.

She founded Girl Connection because she deeply believes in the power of connections, collaboration, change, education, and community. In addition to being the founder of Girl Connection, she is the Chief Visionary Officer of Esther's Court Etiquette Academy, Queen Esther's Court Young ladies mentoring circle and The Purpose Circle Elite Coaching. She works together with women to learn about the nature of her pass and current difficulties, such as any experience of anxiety, sadness, fear, isolation, overwhelm, shame, or confusion, and explore her strengths to facilitate insight and growth. Ms. Williams has two Bachelor's degrees, a certification in stenography and etiquette, a native of Freeport, Bahamas. See more of Laquisha at www.laquishawilliams.com

Wanda Briscoe

Wanda S. Briscoe is an author, entrepreneur, mentor, motivational speaker, and mother of three. In January 2011, she was diagnosed with Breast Cancer. Her life changed forever. In October 2012, Wanda published her first book called "The Fight Within", which focused on the emotional, mental, and spiritual road she traveled while battling the disease. Wanda uses her diagnosis as a platform to educate, inspire, and motivate others. She is a mentor, providing knowledge, support, and encouragement to those who are just beginning to battle Breast Cancer. Wanda is also the co-founder of Forever Eden Organics, a Bath & Body company that specializes in organic products for men, women, and children. See more of Wanda at www.wandabriscoe.org

Find Your Fierce

One day, I had an epiphany which opened my eyes to how I was being held back by my limiting belief that I wasn't good enough. I realized that I had to let go of being so focused on what other people thought about me and what other people said about me. I had to let go of what they said I should do and be and, instead, I really began to define ME for myself.

I remember my epiphany moment; it was back in 1993 while I was in one of the greatest seasons of my life, by everybody else's definition. What I realized in that moment is that I spent years being OK with everyone else's definition of who I should be and what I should do. So when I stopped to define ME for myself, it was at a time when I had built an incredible career in the entertainment industry, working for one of Viacom's largest cable networks. This television network was largely successful, in that we had an outreach to 89 million homes on a weekly basis. From there I was elevated into a Casting Director position with the number one television show on Fox. This job then led me to work with an entertainment group, where together what we produced was responsible for generating over 12.6 billion dollars annually. On top of that I was going to all the "Hot Hollywood Parties." I was bumping elbows with all the stars and dating a few, but at the same time saying to myself, "I don't think this is really who I am. I don't think this is my passion." I had this whisper inside of me saying, "Nicole, there is something bigger waiting for you," but I had no idea what that was!

I remember feeling like I was standing at a fork in the road! A fork that made me look at myself in the mirror and for the first time in my life ask myself, "What do YOU want?" In that moment I was willing to release what everyone had to say I should do and be for my future. I no longer cared about what anyone else thought I should be or do and I began to listen to my heart. I began to follow my gifts and allowed my passion to define my life.

Doing this made me feel alive!! It was in this place that I discovered my power, my FIERCE, and I began to grow me. Matter of fact, it felt so darn good being me, the true and authentic real me, I began to stand unapologetically in me. It felt so wonderful that I wanted every person I knew, every client I had in the entertainment industry, every person I met to feel the same way. It was in this space I realized my life calling was to pour into people who were in the same place I was in, people who were seeking how to truly stand in their truth and own their power!

Because this was such a new place for me, I started seeking out anything I could find to help grow me. I first started reading books. The first one I read was "Woman Thou Art Loosed" by T.D. Jakes, and then there was "Value in the Valley" by Iyanla Vanzant. It was in this season I realized my love of books and continued to order book after book after book to grow me. Next I started to attend conferences and it was the combination of the two, reading and workshops, where I actually began to identify my passion for helping people recognize and define their power and how to stand in it every day. I loved it so much that I really wanted to do this full time as a career. However, this was 20 years ago, when being a life coach was not popular and I had no idea what to call this thing I felt so passionate about doing. Eventually, all my research on how to grow this gift in me led me back to school and I earned a Masters Degree in Social Work. My MSW taught me the skills and tools I needed to work one on one as a personal development coach and to develop programs and curriculum as a curriculum development coach.

Additionally, as I began to grow me, I started attracting people who were in the same plight I was in, people looking to find themselves just I had done years before. This is where my life's work began to connect and I started working to pour into the lives of women.

My Core Message of Activation

Find Your Fierce! Stop hiding behind limits, fears, and doubts to unleash your gifts—stand in your power and make an unstoppable impact in the world. You may ask, what does "Finding Your Fierce" look like? How do I go about activating it? My answer is, create your own FIERCE through learning the skills to own and grow your power, your gift, your greatness, and then learn how that gift becomes your way to serve the world and leave an impact.

As the creator of the **"Find Your Fierce"** formula, I work with women who have a rumble in their bellies to make a big impact in the world, but feel restricted or held back by factors they can't seem to identify, fully comprehend, or conquer on their own. My coaching process enables my clients to "flip the switch" that turns up their power and shines their true essence and light for the world to see. It is this switch that sets a purpose in motion. I do this work as both a content and personal development coach.

Personal development, where you identify any barriers holding you back from fully standing in your power—your FIERCE—and content development, where you put your purpose in motion and unleash your gift into the world to increase your ability to serve all those you are called to touch, move, and inspire.

I personally activated these methods first by discovering that I was playing small and needed to step into activating my own power, and really beginning to grow the inner me. And while my journey, my standing in my purpose and owning my personal power looks like me holding the space for women, your journey is likely altogether different. So what I am saying to you is that activation of your gifts, standing in your truth, and owning your power unapologetically MUST take place to "Find Your Fierce" and build the life of your dreams.

Activation Steps

The one thing you must know is your dream, your gift; your calling is what you were born to do and how you are meant to serve the world! So today is not just a day for you to get inspired again, but a day to find where you must take action to set the wheels in motion toward living your dream. Here are a few steps that can help you do that:

1. **Be Confident** – Know that you already have everything you need. You were birthed with the purpose, the gift, to do or to be something special. All you have to do is… what's the name of this step?
2. **Get Clear and Stay Focused** – What is your purpose? In what way can you fully exercise your gift? What do

you want? You have got to be clear on how you will work to make your dream real in your life. This is why people make vision boards, so they can get clear and stay focused on what they want and will work toward. You can't hit the target if you can't see where you are pointing the arrow.

3. **Make a Plan** – For your clarity, the true key to focus is knowing what action you need to take NOW. Look at where you are today and figure out how you get to where you want to go; what you need to do to get there; how long it will take; how much money you will need, etc.... plan it ALL out.

4. **Be Unapologetic About It** – Stop looking for people to accept your purpose. You validate it and make your own confirmation that you are on the right path. No one is pregnant with your purpose but YOU, so you MUST know it is up to you birth it, to make it real in your life. So move forward without regret, knowing that when your purpose is fully birthed for the world to see, everyone will see exactly what has been burning inside of you.

5. **Grow it** – Find ways to grow your gift. You cannot truly grow to what's possible without continually educating yourself. Whatever your dreams or goals are, I have to tell you as your sister in the journey, you don't know everything it's going to take to actually get there. So ask yourself: **What do I need to learn to get where I want to be?** Growing and learning can look like any of the following:

- Formal education – Bachelor's, Master's, or PhD degrees
- Vocational education – training classes or certification programs
- Reading books, listening to CDs or audio podcasts
- Attending conferences and workshops
- Hiring a coach – someone who can walk through the process with you and help you design and implement what you need to get done
- Finding a mentor – someone who has been there and done that, someone who can share with you and foster your learning

So today I ask you, what ACTION will you take to move yourself toward your dream? What is it that you WILL do? That thing you are dreaming about, thinking about, talking to everybody about—how will you move that into ACTIVATION? The next set of stories will help.

Nicole Roberts Jones

Beauty and the Beast
From Depressed to Driven and The Seeds of Transformation

As I quietly looked back over my life, I began to see the cycle of life repeating itself. My life was playing out the same exact way my mother's had. She began motherhood at the tender age of nineteen when she gave birth to me, and she later had my two younger brothers. I watched her sacrifice her life to take on her role and responsibilities as a mother for my brothers and me. I can only imagine that she had big dreams that she wanted to pursue for her life, but as many of us sometimes do, she packed up her dreams, labeled them, and put them in storage.

I never imagined that I would fall in love at such an early age, although this might be expected of one who had an absent father growing up. I never laid eyes on my real father and my stepfather who lived in our home displayed unhealthy dysfunction. Therefore, I attached my feelings with the first man that came into my life and showed me love. I had just completed high school with the dream of becoming a model (*what happened to that dream? OOPS…it has now been added to my bucket list*).

My husband and I were high school sweethearts. We had just completed our senior year of high school in '92 when we were presented with our very first graduation present: a pregnancy. The plans for our future had taken a dramatic turn. Our dreams were put on hold and we didn't know where to go from there or know how to dream another dream. We went on to get married.

Beauty and the Beast

By the age of twenty-three, I was a wife and a mother of a three-year-old, as well as the manager of our household. He and I knew nothing about being parents, let alone being married, but we learned along the way, step by step and year by year.

We currently have been together for twenty-four years, and have been married for seventeen of them. Although we made it through the statistics of young marriages, the road to happiness has not been an easy one. Throughout our years together, we definitely had our share of happy but also trying times. Having these responsibilities at such a young age caused me to have to grow up fast. I believed that taking on these roles meant I had to put my dreams on hold. This reality would turn out to be the path that I would travel for some years to come. The road I chose was to continually place my hopes and dreams on the back burner in order to support those close to me.

Twenty-three years later…who am I now? Still a wife of seventeen years and a mother of a now twenty-year-old son who is in his junior year of college pursuing his DREAMS. I also have thirteen-year-old twin girls that get my constant attention as I sow wisdom and empower them to pursue their dreams and goals no matter what age they are. I must say I have raised three amazing children over these years despite my challenges and struggles of not knowing who I was or wanted to become. In raising my family, I lost my personal purpose. That is why I stress the importance of dreams and purpose to my children. Every dream or idea that I have ever desired, I didn't think was actually attainable. I mentally packed away all of my dreams and put them in boxes in storage. I know I can't speak for all women, but many of us have done this self-consciously without even noticing that our dreams have died. We'll set a goal to accomplish a dream and what do you know? Here comes a setback, whether it's the birth of a child, divorce, disappointments, etc. It's time to take back what we want!

Throughout the years, I just went through the motions of life. But much to my surprise, in the summer of 2010 I would be shaken by a storm that was so unexpected. What you would call a routine doctor's appointment with concerns of feeling fatigue and body aches would turn my whole world upside down by one statement: "you're suffering from Depression." I was in total denial. "Who, me? Not me! I know God and He wouldn't do this to me." I took this information and researched Depression. The more I read and learned, the deeper the Depression took over my mind and body. I secluded myself from everything and everyone around me. I did a great job of hiding it from my friends and family. The only two who knew the depth of my illness were God and my husband. I questioned God over and over again: "What is happening to me?"

Even though I had a relationship with God, Depression was able to sneak in and take up residence in my mind. I ignored the advice of the doctors to take the anti-depression medication prescribed to me and put on a "happy face" to make those close to me believe I was okay. I tried my best to hide how I was dealing with this from my husband, but he knew better. Other than my husband, no one else realized that inside, I was slowly fading away.

On August 2, 2010, my life changed and would never again be the same. I fell to my knees, weary and in a distressed state of mind. At this point, the Depression had taken over my entire mind and body. (*John 10:10—"The thief cometh not, but for to steal, and to kill, and to destroy."KJV*) I wanted to just give up on life itself at this point and all of the dreams that I hadn't fulfilled. I just didn't care anymore, nor did I want to hurt any more than I was already. As usual, my husband continued to voice his concerns about my mental state. This day was no different than any other. He asked me if I had ever felt like I wanted to harm myself. I replied with confidence, "No, I don't feel like I want to do any harm to myself." I proceeded to drop him off at work, and I headed back home to get some rest. Rest and sleep were really hard to come by at that time. I suffered from many restless nights, oftentimes never sleeping at all. I tried to lie down and rest, but a rested mind was far from was what I got. My mind began wandering and I heard a very loud voice in my head tell me, "Just kill yourself." I jumped from the bed, trembling with fear at what I had just heard. Then another still voice came in my head and said, "Call your family and tell them that you love them." I remember calling my husband in such a frantic panic and crying out to him, sharing what I had experienced. At the same time, I began to call upon my heavenly Father for help. I realized that I could no longer battle this demon on my own and remembered God knows exactly what we need when we need it!

With all the weeping, a shift came over me as I cried out to God. I fell to my knees and began to call out to Him, begging for help. "I can't do this on my own. Not my might, but by Your might. I know there is more that You shall have me do, God." That is what I began confessing, out loud, with my mouth. I can't explain it but through prayer, encouragement, and therapy, God has raised me up out of that dark place and brought life, dreams, and vision back into my life.

I share this little part of my life with you to let you know that no matter what SETBACK, OBSTACLE, ROAD BLOCK, or POTHOLE comes your way on your road to destiny, GOD IS ABLE! For the first time in my life, I can say God had transformed me and renewed my mind so that I can begin to live out the life He has designed for me. I didn't understand the process and everything that I was going through, so I fought it. When I realized what lesson God was trying to reveal to me, an *Ah-Ha*! Moment happened. Instead of having a woe-is-me attitude, or a *why is this happening to me?* moment, I truly allowed the transformation and the renewing of my mind to fully take root in my life. As a result, I started to see my life flourish. My dreams were re-ignited and I swiftly became the *CEO of my dreams.*

What are the dreams and desires you have for your future? Maybe you have had some big dreams, but things didn't go the way you planned. So you packed up all your dreams and put them in a box and you forgot all about them. Well, we've all had some disappointments and setbacks that allowed us to forget about our dreams. But today is a new day and we serve a God who makes all things new and possible.

I challenge you today to dig deep and unpack those dreams and live them out on purpose with purpose. When one dream dies, dream another dream. There's nothing you can dream that God can't do. Trust that He is working behind the scenes on your behalf. Remember to dare to believe and dare to dream another dream, because God desires to do BIG things in and through us!

I encourage you to dedicate ten to fifteen minutes of each day to engage yourself with lessons. I have prepared exercises, activities, strategies, and tips that helped me reinvent and transform my life. Each lesson will leave you inspired and empowered to start visualizing what you want and to start executing your dreams. Go for it!

DREAM IT…CREATE IT…EXECUTE IT!
Activation Lesson:
Visualize one of your dreams
Daily Confession…
I AM *moving one step closer into the direction of my vision*

Only those who see the invisible can achieve the impossible. Belief in your vision is the key to creating your own destiny. First you must taste your vision, touch your vision, feel your vision, emotionalize your vision, and finally own your vision. The "how" of making it happen will slowly present itself.

Visualize every single detail:

When you visualize a goal or a dream, make sure you visualize all possible details. For example, visualize yourself moving into your dream home. Begin seeing in your mind what each room looks like; see how the furniture and curtains will look. The more detailed your dream is, the more passionate you will become about making it happen.

My Vision:

At one point in my life, visualizing my dreams was very hard to do. I would get stuck on what was happening in my life at that particular moment and I couldn't see past it. I would be the visionary for everyone else's dreams, and helped those around me put their dreams into perspective. I decided to shift some things around and begin to visualize what I wanted to do. I started journaling about what I wanted to come to pass in my life.

Nuggets to live by:

See the invisible and you can achieve the impossible

Fill your mind with visual pictures

Don't get stuck in the moment

Activate Your Journey:

I encourage you to begin to write out your vision and what that would look like for your life.

Example: I am healthy, happy, and whole.

What is your vision? Write it out in your journal. See the below example

Daily Confession…

***I AM** writing out my visions and making them clear*

Every second, minute, and hour you have a thought, write it down. Carry a journal with you. Some of your best ideas will happen when you least expect it and you don't want them to be forgotten. Every morning before you do anything, write down whatever is on your mind. So many ideas come to light after you have had plenty of rest. Try using music to help you become more relaxed, motivated, or focused, then use it while visualizing your goals and dreams.

My Personal Journey of Activation:

My twin daughters and I were out shopping one day and one of them came over to me with this pink journal in her hands. On the cover of this journal was a silhouette of a woman in a dress beautiful with the words *"Be Fabulous"* on it. My daughter knew I would fall in love with it, so of course it came home with me. From that moment on, I began journaling and writing down all of the things I wanted to accomplish.

Nuggets to live by:

Use music to relax and meditate

Remember that a relaxed mind brings fresh ideas

Carry a journal to take notes

Your Journey of Activation:

Start writing down a list of things that your want to accomplish. Start with writing out your plan. This will allow you to have a clearer vision of what you want to accomplish

Tameika McPhaul

Choosy Lover
Bad Girl Gone Graciously Good

BAD

The word bad is described in many ways: *not good in any manner or degree; not achieving an adequate standard; poor;* and *unfavorable.*

BAD THOUGHTS

You are stupid. You will never amount to anything. No one will ever love you. You can't change your life. Everybody will laugh at you. You are a loser. You should have known. All men are alike. So what if he is disrespectful to you; that's his way of showing love. Happiness is an illusion.

Life is funny. It amazes me how it always has something to teach you. Paying attention to it reaps a wealth of knowledge that goes beyond common understanding. Before my situation, I didn't get that people come into your life for a reason, a season, or a lifetime. But as I sit here and think back… I would not change a thing.

I USED TO…

Think my heart was invincible from being hurt. I was the one who did the heartbreaking. I never thought about the consequences of my behavior nor did I consider the feelings of others. When I look back at the things I have said and done, my thought life, and my "get them before they get you" attitude towards men, it amazes me to see the woman that I am now.

The moment that changed my life came from attending a particular event at the Jacob Javits Center. Iyanla Vanzant was speaking and her powerful message made me take a deep look within myself to find out *who am I?* I will never forget picking up her book "One Day My Soul Opened Up" and how it gave me insight on life and developing my personal relationship with God. I remember it clearly. I was on a spiritual journey that didn't involve an entourage. Just me and the Creator.

It was that personal relationship with God that made me want more than random "friendships" or relationships with men. I desired a helpmate and when the perfect-looking man came along, I thought he was it.

LOVE OF HIM...

He was different. Well-educated. Parents well-to-do. He was college-educated, a working man who had a different kind of game. "I am going to marry her" is what he told a colleague of mine about me. Of all the dudes I have met and all of the lines I have heard, I had never heard this. He piqued my interest by telling me all the things I wanted to hear, using buzz words like "marriage," "God," and "family," and since I was at the beginning of developing my personal relationship with God, I naturally thought "this could be it." *Oh God, give me a sign to show me that he is the one.*

His words played on the strings of my heart—the same heart that desired to be married, the same heart that had never been broken. *Is he the one to take this bad girl and make her good? Could he be the one that God sent my way?* Oh, the thoughts that engulfed my head.

For three years I participated in an on-and-off-again "relationship" that I led myself to believe would lead to the desires of my heart: to get married and have a family. But during these three years, he exhibited behavior that was not consistent with that of a man who wanted to settle down. He would say "I love you" and then wouldn't call for days. He would say "I miss you" and then not be available for us to see each other. But because I wanted this thing called love to work; I would make excuses for his behavior. "Oh, he is working so hard—that is why he is unavailable," I would say. During the times we did get to spend together, he made sure he was acting in a loving and kind way. This included showering me with gifts, telling me how great and understanding I was, and telling me I was the only one who understood him. I was hooked and nothing else seemed to matter. But I always asked, "Oh, God, just give me a sign to let me know that he is the man for me." Little did I know God *was* giving me signs; I just wasn't paying attention. I was doing my own thing.

I remember first introducing him to my brother, who said as clear as day, "He is cheating on you." I was so upset with my brother. He didn't know this man from a hole in the wall and yet he was telling me that my boyfriend was cheating on me. I made a mental note never to speak about him to my brother again! I didn't need my brother's negative energy on this "great love" of mine. He is my younger brother! What does he know about love?

NOW I DON'T...

It was a couple of hours before my twenty-seventh birthday. I felt quiet inside, possibly because I felt old or possibly because I didn't have any plans. My birthday was on a Friday and I felt obligated to do something. My original plans to head to Vegas were interrupted by my fear of flying. I blamed 9/11 for that. My girlfriends made plans for me but we were not going out until Saturday. My boyfriend told me we would do something on Friday, but he had been unpredictable and hadn't been keeping his word. And then he called.

It was my birthday and I wanted to see him. He called and we made plans to go to dinner. I would meet him at his house and off we would go. These past three years on and off had been a real-life roller coaster, but oh, *I just love me some of him.* Or so I thought.

I got to his house, but all the lights were off, and clearly no one was home, so I called him. "I'm on my way. I will be there in ten minutes," he said. Ten minutes turned to twenty, and twenty turned to two hours. I must be some kind of fool. Was I so desperate to sit in a car waiting on this man who has done nothing but blow smoke for the longest time? Thoughts of self-doubt began to flood my head. There was that voice again, saying, "You are stupid. You are the worst." And yet I still sat in my car, hungry, tired, and cramping. I remember hearing my good girl voice saying GO HOME, but I ignored her. It was my birthday and I wanted to see him. I wanted to have a good time. Who sits at home alone on her birthday? Not me! *GO HOME!* I heard again. I felt the nudging in my spirit telling me to get out of there. "Oh, just a few more minutes," I thought. I thought that maybe if I had a drink it would make the waiting easier.

So I decided to make a quick stop at the liquor store, thinking he would be there by the time I got back. But no such luck. I became more impatient and then he finally drove up and flashed his smile. The smile that seemed to wear me down before words even came out of his mouth. He apologized, telling me some story that I wanted to believe, but it didn't sit well. And again I heard: *GO HOME.* I ignored that voice; it always wanted to ruin my fun. After all, he showed up, right? So what if it was two hours later?

By then, it was too late to go to the restaurant where we planned on going, so he said we would go to breakfast in the morning. We fell asleep, and then I woke up to the doorbell ringing. I turned to see if he was still in bed, but he was gone. The dog was barking, and then the telephone began to ring. In my mind, something was not right; maybe it was the stillness in the house, or maybe it was my mind playing tricks on me. My heart began to beat faster as the beep from the answering machine allowed the caller to leave a message. "I know you are in there," belted a female's voice. "I see her car out here! Answer the door!" This girl was not playing. She wanted to get in the house, she was mad, and then there was a second beep as the answering machine cut her off. I started to pack my stuff, my mind racing. What was I going to do? He wasn't here and she was outside. Would I have to fight? The bad girl in my head said, "Be prepared to fight!" The other voice said, "Be calm; you are not an animal or that girl who is out of control. I told you to go home last night."

I packed up my stuff, put my shoes on, and headed towards the door. What was I going to do? Who was this girl outside his house? I grabbed the doorknob, opened the door, and the sun was at its brightest. I took a deep breath walked out the door, heart now racing and thumping. I exhaled and said, "Who are you?" As she spoke, I felt like I was in a fog, and when I came out of it, all I remember hearing was, "I'm his fiancée." By that point, I was having an out-of-body experience. I was very calm as I asked her some questions. The one answer I distinctly remember is that they had been engaged for eight months!

As both of us stood outside the house, she gave me all the details about their up-and-down cheating relationship, and while she told me everything I did not want to hear, my whole being became numb. I was in total shock to think that he had been living this double life, lying to me and putting me in the worst position. Words could not express what I was feeling: betrayed, caught in a web of lies, heart-broken, you name it.

She tried to call him and get him to come to the house to talk to both of us, but of course he never came. So many thoughts were running through my mind. I had believed in him and our relationship. I knew that I was feeling as if he wasn't ready to be in a committed relationship, that he had issues he needed to deal with, but I had no idea it was to this magnitude. And in that moment, my brother's voice echoed in my head: "He is cheating on you." As I zoned in and out of our conversation, I heard her say she had seen my car parked at his house several times, but he always had a story and like me, she, too, was in love and wanted to believe the stories he had been selling.

I gathered my things, reached out to this woman, and gave her a hug! I know it sounds crazy, but I did. This woman and I did not exchange insults. We did not eyeball each other down. What we did do was see that we were both in the same boat, placed in a situation by a man who had no concept of self-love or respect. We both were equally hurt, although she voiced hers more than I did. Maybe it was my defense mechanism—maybe I was still in shock—but when I left her in front of his house, I gave her the tightest hug. You would have thought she and I were old friends. I embraced her because she was his fiancée and had to deal with whether or not to go through with her wedding. I embraced her because all too often, women fight each other over men but on that day, that would not be my role. I embraced her because it was my way of accepting the final sign that showed me this man was not the man God had for me.

When he finally called me, he was mumbling things that I could barely make out. He seemed to be apologetic but my mind was not ready to hear that. I needed to work towards healing from this "relationship." I found myself being encouraged by a Lauryn Hill song featuring Mary J. Blige: "I Used to Love Him, But Now I Don't." The words in this song resonated with me all too well. It was as if she took a snapshot of my life and put into words the very things I was going through. I begged for God to give me a clue or hint that would show me the lessons in this madness.

And then God said, "Let there be light!"

Healing from a broken or toxic relationship is not a small feat. When you give your time, heart, and soul to someone, moving on does not happen overnight.

In the beginning, I was searching for the lesson in this chaos. I knew there was one but I just could not figure it out. I was going into a "valley." I was numb and really prevented myself from feeling anything. I mean, in my head I knew I was hurt, but the tears didn't come—only anger. I was angry with myself for trusting him, especially because there were indicators that suggested he was not being truthful.

I thought it would take a while for me to gain understanding, but as soon as I asked "why?" the answers came running. And here is the revelation:

- I believed that because I cheated in the past, I was a bad girl and deserved any wrong thing that happened to me.
- I wanted to be a girlfriend so badly that it didn't matter if he was not ready. I wanted to prove I could be loyal and take care of a man.
- I wanted to change him into what I imagined my husband to be, even when his actions didn't mimic what I needed.
- I wanted to have a boyfriend to talk about with my friends.
- His actions showed me he was not ready, even though I persisted and told myself he was.

After all of this came to me, I felt much lighter. I had tears in my eyes because learning the truth about yourself is some kind of experience. I knew he had issues and so did I. I forgave him and learned to let go of any anger I had been feeling. He lied to me because I lied to myself. And while my heart was warm for him, I prayed that someday he would work through his own pain. I'm not judging him. After experiencing the loss of someone I loved and who I thought loved me, I did what I needed to do: TOOK CARE OF ME! This included smiling and learning to love unconditionally.

At the time, I was reminded of God's love for me, that love that put me in a good place. I did not know for sure what He had in store for me, but I did know that whatever it was, it was for my highest good. I spent my alone time "dating myself" and developing my relationship with God. It was a time of reflection, peace, and no chaos. Today, I have a wonderful family and am married to a wonderful man who treats me like the queen that I am. My break-up may have broken me down, but this thing that was bad graciously led me into something good. I started focusing on my career and following my purpose in life to empower women and girls to see their self-worth and believe all things are possible. I started sharing my testimony and showing others that your trials in life do not define you; it's how your rise from the ashes like a Phoenix that will be your legacy. I could not make someone love me like I deserved to be loved, but what I did do was love myself enough to recognize when enough was enough. By the time I met my husband, I was in a good place - A place where I surrendered my hopes and dreams over to the Creator - A place where love was overflowing - a place where what I wanted in life was limitless.

Activation Steps

Self-Love

How do you feel about yourself? Take a minute to look in the mirror and say, "I Love You! I love everything about you. You are a pretty big deal!" Take time to learn about who you are. In a journal, jot down your hopes and dreams, your likes and dislikes. Start to speak life to yourself. This is the prime time to work on your personal and spiritual development. Your life journey is all about self-discovery. Your worth is valued far above rubies! You deserve the best. Every morning when you wake up, have an attitude of thanks, despite what happened the night before. Train your mind to think positive thoughts. When negative thoughts try to enter your mind, counter them by saying, "but God loves me." Release yourself from anything that makes you feel less than who you were born to be. Give fear an eviction notice. Make a decision to not allow your fears to hold you hostage.

Enjoy Yourself

Make a list of things you want to do and start living from that list. Take yourself to the movies and out to the finest restaurants. Adorn yourself with nice things. Focus on the things that make you happy. At the same time, recognize the things that cause you pain and sadness. Work through those feelings and emotions by being honest with yourself.

Relationships

We have been bombarded with false images of what love is supposed to look like and, at times, have put our integrity and self-worth on the chopping block. But the truth is, being in a healthy relationship takes work. You have to know the value you bring to the table as well as appreciate the value your partner brings to the table. Everything you want in a relationship starts with the relationship you have with yourself. If you are not being treated like the queen God created you to be, then you have to take an honest look at the relationship. Work on saying yes to a relationship that is reciprocal. Maya Angelou said, "When somebody shows you who they are, believe them." The man I was with presented himself well; however, his actions were a contradiction to everything he said to me. Think about it this way: if you had to talk to your child about being in a relationship, what would you say? What type of man or woman would you hope for? If you as a loving parent want these things for your child, imagine what the Creator wants for you!

Everything you want in life begins with your thought process. Learning how to combat negative thoughts about yourself will help you in all areas of your life, whether in relationships, finances, your career, etc. It all begins with how you see yourself and what you believe you can achieve.

Fatima Scipio

From Pieces to Peace
Recovering a Sense of Identity

According to *Webster's Dictionary*, the word "true" means "agreeing with the facts: not false; to be real or genuine." As a child, I grew up in an abusive household where truth was not allowed. In place of truth, there was a great deal of secrecy and darkness. Secrecy surrounding ten years of emotional and physical abuse was created by the hands of my father. "You're stupid and dumb like your mother; you will never amount to anything," was my truth for many years of my life. I endured a wealth of emotional beat-downs and occasional smacks and poundings on my body starting at age six. The abuse I endured was so severe I was sure the day would come when my father would kill me. And if that day arrived, my death would not have been due to the abuse, but because of the silence of others.

The abuse became so harsh that I attempted suicide while in the seventh grade. In my mind, death was far better than what I was experiencing at home. I couldn't understand why God wouldn't take me out of my misery. I had so many questions but no answers.

At age sixteen, I was finally able to escape my father and place myself in the foster care system. Once in foster care, I struggled with finding the "truth", -my truth. Being in foster care didn't make that task any easier. Because the media only focuses on the negative stories that come out of foster care, the word "care" has an unfavorable stigma in the term "foster care."

I developed much insecurity while being in the system. Since I had very low self-esteem, it was easy to wear the labels society had given me: a reject, a menace to society, another statistic, and the list goes on.

Entering foster care made me bitter and angry, and I felt like the world was against me. I wanted everyone I came in contact with to pay for the pain I endured as a child. But I would settle for becoming an attorney one day and putting away every parent that abused their child. I convinced myself that life wasn't fair and that I was a victim. As a child I had been taught that vulnerability was a sign of weakness, so I became numb. My heart was closed and black. I was mean, rude, entitled, and a bully. I operated from a place of hate instead of love. It was easier to be on automatic and be disconnected. After all, that is how I had spent most of my life: fight or flight. I had been operating in life or death mode, so there was never time to think before I acted. I was always living in reaction. I felt like a dead man walking, present in the physical form, but checked out of life a long time earlier. I needed to find my way amongst the living again.

What I didn't realize was that the life I had lived wasn't supporting me or helping me reach my goals. The way I was showing up in the world and in my relationships wasn't working at all, but I wasn't open to doing anything about it. I took pride in living a mediocre life. My ego hadn't suffered enough for me to believe I had to try something different.

I've learned many lessons through my pain and suffering. A part of me is ashamed of the person I used to be, but the other part of me is grateful for that period of time because it has made me the woman I am today. After all, isn't this how we learn in life—through experience?

Since my father raised me to believe that I was "stupid and dumb" like my mother, I sought answers from other people, not realizing what I was seeking was inside of me the whole time. I was very anxious, and defensive. I didn't have the confidence to walk through life effectively. I was always second-guessing myself and didn't know how to handle certain situations. This resulted in giving my power of choice to others. I allowed others to dictate who I was; I wore their labels and believed I was who they told me I was- "angry, rude, dramatic and a failure." Everyone's lack of confidence and support made me believe that I wasn't worthy, so I chose to walk through life ANGRY. Actually, angry is an understatement—I was more or less pissed the f*** off at the world. Inside of the anger was my hurt, but I didn't want to admit it. After all, I was raised to not feel any type of pain or show any emotions, and this is how I navigated through life… emotionless and numb. Hearing that I would never amount to anything without my father and that no man would ever want me were words that started to grow like seeds inside my heart. I had low self-esteem and no confidence. I merely existed, as opposed to living life.

My anger led me to a love affair with alcohol that had me two steps away from AA. I suffered a mental breakdown during my college career in 2003 which resulted in me taking a leave of absence from school. I was reckless and irresponsible. All of this forced me to do something I said I would never do: slow down. Taking time off from school led me to a therapist who supported me in dealing with the things I had been running from most of my adult life. It was time to deal with the reality of my mother abandoning me and having to be raised by an abusive father. I had reached a point where I could no longer run or hide anymore.

In 2010, I reached a different type of low in my life. I had accomplished so much but wasn't happy and was STILL very angry. I had dreams of becoming an attorney and making a difference for children in the foster care system, but I was afraid to pursue my dream. I was in relationships with people because of the fear of being alone. A part of me knew this was not what life was supposed to be like. However, reaching my lowest point meant that there was nowhere to go but up. This meant I had to be open to doing something different in order to get different results in my life. Plus, I needed to gain clarity on what my purpose was.

One day a dear friend of mine called me up and introduced me to the world of transformational work. I attended a series of workshops that taught me things I never knew were possible. I learned that I MATTERED. I realized that I was operating from a place of scarcity in different areas of my life, including the relationships I had. Attending these workshops and putting the tools into application was very powerful for me. This work, also known as "self-development work," is something I am grateful for every day of my life. Everything and anything I once thought was impossible suddenly became possible because I had the tools to create the life I wanted and attract the type of people I wanted in my life.

Through these workshops I realized the need to ask myself certain questions. I found the courage to dig deeper and search for answers to important questions I never took time to ask. What would make me happy? What did I want? As I continued to dig within myself I learned that I never really wanted to become an attorney. The driving force behind all of my accomplishments was to seek revenge on my father. I wanted to prove him wrong and show him that I would be someone one day. I was pursuing the wrong career for the wrong reasons. Being an attorney wasn't what was truly in my heart. It didn't feel right in my spirit. But everyone else thought it was what was best for me. So along with proving my father wrong and being a people-pleaser, I convinced myself that becoming an attorney was the only way to make "decent" money and make a difference in the lives of foster children.

Through my journey, struggles, and pain, I have finally found the meaning of the word "true." To me, TRUE really stands for:

Trust that the answers lie within you
Rest assured; you are the creator of your experiences
Use your pain to support others and be in contribution to society
Emerge into your highest possibility

I will admit I was skeptical about exploring "new possibilities" through the workshops I took. I thought I knew all the answers to life, and because of my insecurities, I was an arrogant, hurtful, and a mean person. I used my arrogance as a mask so people wouldn't know how insecure and scared I really was. My arrogance wouldn't allow me to be open to new possibilities or admit to myself that I didn't have all the answers. I was hardly open to the idea that there was still SO much more to learn. I had major trust issues that paralyzed me in different ways and showed up in different areas of my life. My anger was like a time bomb waiting to go off, and I was always desperately trying to figure out whether to cut the red wire or the blue one before it exploded.

My experience with transformational work had me feeling EMPOWERED. Many things opened up for me. I learned a lot about myself and how I was showing up in the world. I learned that my intentions had to be in alignment with my actions. I had to say "x" and do "x" as opposed to saying "x" and doing "y." For many years, I had the habit of keeping folks in my life that had been there during my darkest time simply because of what they had done for me, as opposed to focusing on what they were currently bringing to our relationship. I learned that was no longer working for me. It was time for me to stop ignoring what was in my heart and take action about the people who were in my life. I learned people treat you the way you allow them to, and I was allowing people to walk all over me and treat me poorly. Then I had the nerve to act like a victim about it instead of speaking what was in my heart. I had friends who weren't keeping their promises to me, and not being in integrity. They felt they had the right to be lazy when it came to things I needed or requested from them. It made me question why I was surrounded by these kinds of people. Then I realized it was because I wasn't living with integrity. I wasn't being TRUE to myself. I shrunk myself because it made others feel good. I was acting small in life because those around me felt comfortable and I needed them to continue to like me.

For many years, I couldn't understand why God kept me alive that day when I finally escaped my father. I started to question certain events in my life. Why didn't my father kill me that day? Why was I so guarded and disconnected? Why was I so ANGRY? I didn't realize that a lot of my experiences had affected me and were showing up in many areas of my life that I wasn't even aware of. After beginning my journey, transformational work gave me the tools to help me unlock the answers to some of my burning questions. I was finally able to navigate through all of these questions and get to the source. It allowed me to peel away the layers and years of hurt until I reached... myself. And so I did. I peeled away layers upon layers of anger and hurt and layers that just weren't working in my life anymore, and in doing so, I rediscovered myself.

I gained confidence that allowed me to go after my passion and start to create the life I dreamed about. I realized I could become wealthy and still make a difference in the lives of members in the foster care community as a public speaker, life coach, and writer. Helping others by using my story is part of my journey. It is all part of God's assignment for me, and instead of running away from it as I had before, I am now running towards it. I have a purpose and part of it is to share my story of triumph and to impact as many lives as possible. I've learned we ALL have purpose. We are ALL here for a reason. I get to use my experience to be in contribution to others. At the end of the day, we are connected and all have a story that can support someone else who is experiencing something similar. The thing that hurts us the most is often the story that can help others most.

Many people in the world have used their pain to inspire others. So I decided I wanted to be one of those people. I always heard how people "created" their reality. But I had never understood what that meant. It took a while for me to realize that I am the creator and the author of my life. I was creating the good and bad things that were manifesting. Once I learned the tools to better equip myself and create what I wanted, I became unstoppable. I began to bring forth only the things I wanted and would be forwarding to myself and those around me. In the beginning it was great and I was excited, but then I learned in order to reach my destination this meant getting rid of certain folks in my life. So, I chose... me. I realized certain people no longer served me or were the types of people I wanted to be surrounded by. They were bleeding me dry either through their negative energy or mistreatment towards our friendship. People are a blessing, a lesson as they come into your life for a reason or a season and I needed to know when that season was over.

As I learned to let go of the people and things that were no longer working in my life I needed to create a space where I was allowed to be ME. But first I had to find out who I was. For many years, I was "being my story" instead of moving past it. I was being a child of abuse, a victim. That was who I was. Through transformational work, I am now able to find my authentic self, and choose to be a connected, powerful and loving leader. Again, I am being my AUTHENTIC self without any apologies. And I am grateful every day for that choice.

Through self-development, I found the confidence to operate from a place of love. I learned how to trust the right people and gained confidence that the answers I seek are all within me. For the first time, I choose to live life as opposed to just existing. I am excited for what tomorrow will bring because I am the one creating it. I learned that I am powerful and capable of more than I ever dreamed of and for once am excited about this beautiful thing called life, the good and the bad. I created new relationships with family members who I didn't know existed until a year ago. I have friends who love and accept me as is and hold me to the highest possibility. I finally understand that life is not a rehearsal; we only get one try and if we do it right, once is really all we need. Though this is only the beginning, I am so excited as I continue my journey through transformational work. I look forward to learning more, creating more, and living the life I dream of.

Activation Steps

GO EXPERIENCE SELF DEVELOPMENT WORK—No, really. I would offer that self-development is the gift that keeps giving. It is powerful beyond anything you'll ever experience and will be the best investment you can make in yourself and those who surround you. If you are really committed to living the life you dream of, learning new tools through self-development will support you in making those dreams come true and allow you to show up powerfully in the world. In order to get a different result in your life, you must be willing to do something differently. What are you willing to do in order to have the life you truly want?

If you are currently going through something right now, take the time to reflect on your current situation. Try your best to understand and see how you created this situation, whether through your actions, energy, or thoughts on a conscious or unconscious level. Ask yourself where you can take responsibility for your actions and then figure out what you are committed to doing differently moving forward. Remember, through every breakdown comes breakthrough. Every setback is a setup for your comeback.

Really take a moment to assess the people in your life. Are your relationships give-and-take? Are you surrounded by a bunch of takers? Are both of you supporting one another in the relationship? Are they treating you the way you want to be treated not the way they think they should be treating you? Are they showing up for you like you are showing up for them? Is their energy draining you or propelling you? Are they negative or positive people? Have you been clear about what your expectations are and are they being met? Really dig deep within yourself to ask yourself these questions and then take a course of action that is right for YOU!

What masks do you hide behind? Is it a mask of humor, sarcasm? Ask yourself if wearing this mask is supporting you. If not, what are you willing to do differently in order to remove the mask and show up powerfully in the world as your authentic self?

Are you truly living the life you dream about? Or are you allowing fear and the story you've made up to stand in the way of you and your dream? Write down what brings you joy, and passion. What makes you come alive? Are you currently doing that in your career? Once you've written that down ask yourself are you doing the things on your list in your current career? If the answer is no then come up with an action plan to work towards incorporating those things and truly living the life you want.

Don't be afraid to live the life you dream about. Dream BIG and BOLD, be that next president, invent that next groundbreaking technology, be the next history maker. If not you, then who? If not now, then when? Remember that everything and anything is possible…

Be. Do. Have. But most of all, be TRUE to you.

Pamela Campbell

Contributors

Nicole Roberts Jones

Nicole Roberts Jones is known as "The Inner Catalyst" for her ability to draw out what's best within each of her clients—to inspire, empower and transform them. As the creator of the *Find Your Fierce Formula*, Nicole works with women who have a rumble in their belly to make a big impact in the world, but feel restricted or held back by factors they can't seem to identify, fully comprehend or conquer on their own. Nicole's coaching process enables her clients to "flip the switch" that turns up their power and shines their true essence and light for the world to see.

Nicole works alongside Lisa Nichols and the Motivating the Masses team as Director of Development. She received her Master of Social Work (MSW) from the University of Southern California and has been an adjunct professor at the University of Southern California-School of Social Work and the Boston University School of Social Work. In 2007, Jones was a recipient of the Best of You Award from *Glamour* Magazine and in March of 2011, she was named as one of ten finalists for the National Black Books Festival New Author Award for her 2010 released book *Define Your Own Way*. See more of Nicole at www.nicolerobertsjones.com

Tameika McPhaul

Tameika is the creator of Driven Dream Girl which teaches women and teens how to embrace their ideas and manifest their visions one goal at a time. Through experience, education and insight, Tameika has equipped herself with the necessary tools and resources to make a different in her life and the lives of those around her. She is the author of "Confessions of a Glamfident Woman.", a book of affirmations to uplift and inspire women to confess the positive. See more of Tameika at www.facebook.com/tameika.mcphaul

Fatima Scipio
She is the CEO of Young Enterprising Sisters an entrepreneurial program for girls ages 8-17 that educates, empowers and energizes the next generation of business owners/entrepreneurs.
Fatima is the author of "Boss Lady" (Seven life principles to reign in the new economy) and "First Aid for First Year Teachers" (A practical guide for urban educators). She is owner of New Society Commercial Cleaning and advisory board member of the Yvonne McCalla Foundation, a breast cancer awareness organization that educates young women about early detection and annually offers scholarships to minority women interested in nursing. She has been featured on News12 New Jersey, Redbook magazine, Young Mogul Life Magazine, Vista Magazine, CNN.com and a contributor blogger on the Huffington post.
Fatima received a Bachelor of Science degree in sociology from Virginia State University and her Master of Science degree in urban affairs from Hunter College in New York City. A native of New York, Fatima currently resides in New Jersey, is a wife and the proud mother of one son. See more of Fatima www.fatimascipio.com

Pamela Campbell
One of Pamela's favorite quotes is "You never know how strong you are until being strong is the only choice you have." – Author Unknown. Born in the Ivory Coast of Africa, Pamela came to the United States as a young child. At the age of 16, she was forced to enter Foster Care due to abuse in the home.

After completing high school and attending John Jay College of Criminal Justice, Pamela decided she give back and serve children in Foster Care to protect, encourage and mentor them. Ms. Campbell is the author of upcoming book entitled "A World Apart: From Foster Care to Freedom." See more of Pamela at www.facebook.com/pamela.j.campbell.7

Women Are Powerful!

I remember my day of freedom like it was yesterday. I began consciously releasing people and things that no longer nurtured my purpose. This one simple act inspired me to explore motivation through books, prayer, people I admired, and my amazing church family. Over the years I have built a support system that keeps me balanced, accountable, and most importantly, is trustworthy.

My Core Message of Activation

Women Are Powerful! I believe that I am every woman and every woman is me. Together we are POWERFUL! We must look in the mirror and tell ourselves this daily. Why? Because what we believe in our heart and soul will manifest in our lives. My core values are Sacred Sisterhood, Soul Wealth, and Spiritual Growth sprinkled with compassion, abundance, and authenticity. These things keep me ACTIVATED!

Activation Steps

1. Practice EXTREME self-care.
2. Pursue excellence intentionally! It will help you become the change you want to see and grow you personally.
3. Positively transform! It will allow you to attract the people in your life who are doing the same.

4. Live in your power and trust the God in others. Powerful women don't give time to what they cannot control. There is too much work to be done and enough for each of us.

Now that we have established that you are "powerful," walk in it with a renewed mind which will lead to a bright future. The following stories are about women who had to step up to walk in authenticity, embrace transformation, and accept the greatness within. Each of them is not only powerful…but power FILLED!

Vikki Johnson

A Love Affair
Loving You is Easy Because You Are Beautiful

"She could never go back and make some of the details pretty. All she could do was move forward and make the whole beautiful."
-Terri St. Cloud

Lisa was beautiful, sensual, and connected with her feminine power. With her olive skin, dark hair flowing in waves around her face and shoulders, and almond-colored eyes, she entranced people from many different cultures. Lisa was bold and confident in herself, making eye contact with everyone, lighting up the room with grace and beauty. She loved to play and would dance for hours and hours. Lisa had some short-term and long-term relationships in her life; few were very deep and meaningful, most others were fun for a time. She was a free spirit, a hippie in a new millennial time, someone out of place in this world of dark hearts and sarcastic attitudes. Lisa always saw the bright side of things and was a constant seeker of new experiences, new knowledge, and new relationships. Who wouldn't love Lisa?

Maria was a mother of two and wife of her college sweetheart. She was a humble yet powerful mom who didn't spend much time on her looks. Maria's clothes were both unassuming and baggy as she went about her day with hair pulled back, barely brushed and almost never wearing makeup. Most people didn't notice; she had such kind eyes and a peaceful, calming presence. Her dry, cracked hands were rarely cared for properly because she was too busy. Maria was involved in the Parent-Teacher Association (PTA) as well as other school committees. Her children were well-liked and she knew all of their teachers and staff at the school. Maria had a housekeeper and a nanny to help keep things together. Martha Stewart was one of her idols and she loved watching cooking and lifestyle shows to expand her culinary and home organization skills. She had so much fun being with her children and enjoyed time with her husband as they made plans for their present and future. She was a loving and devoted wife, mother, daughter, sister, aunt, niece, cousin, and granddaughter. Who wouldn't love Maria?

Alex was a powerful leader and manager who wore heels and stood back so that she could look everyone in the eye. She was exotic and petite but strong, wearing black or brown power suits that expressed her confidence. The only flair of color Alex permitted herself came in the form of her shirts, which were normally blue, white, or red. Her poise in any situation was noteworthy and her presence in meetings was a sight to behold. Alex led teams and earned degrees and certifications, along with multiple promotions. She volunteered with professional organizations and participated on nonprofit boards. She led workshops, worked to develop her skills, started businesses, and acquired investment property. She created a small empire of income streams. Alex travelled often to negotiate and improve relationships with business partners for her company. She gained attention from the movers and shakers in her organization and loved talking about business strategy, process, and delivering results. Corporate jets, expense accounts, negotiations, and management strategies were everyday topics for her. She was so dedicated to changing the world and corporate culture in every encounter. Whether in business meetings or on the non-profit organizations' boards, Alex made teams more connected. She had the ability to make leaders more open to hearing diverse opinions without feeling like their status or authority was threatened. Her laugh was contagious and she made people feel like anything was possible when we all worked together. Who wouldn't love Alex?

Who wouldn't love all three of these women? They were amazing, dedicated women who made a difference in many aspects of their lives. But I, for one, did not love them. In fact, I hated them because I knew they were horrible people. They were all liars, frauds, and pretenders who portrayed perfect lives to the public while their private lives were a living hell. Deep down, they felt alone, were struggling to survive, and carrying all their burdens by themselves. Lisa was a drunk and a whore. She had outside relationships with "friends" and created multiple justifications for her choices. At 100 pounds overweight, Maria was a horrible mother and wife who ignored the house and spent more time watching television about cooking than actually cooking. She and her husband lived like roommates in their own home and her kids weren't doing well in school. Alex was in way over her head at work, struggling just to keep up with emails, much less major negotiations. Her business and investment properties bled money every month and were managed poorly. How do I know all of this about them?

Because they were ME.

Each description represented how I would act depending on the situation. I was living all of those lives. Nobody in any of these worlds knew one another, so it was easy to keep them separated in my mind and action. My friends at the club didn't know anyone I worked with, and the school parents and teachers were only seen at school functions. For a while I managed, actually enjoyed, all of the chaos. I thought of myself as a chameleon, adjusting to my surroundings and blending in seamlessly. But it wasn't sustainable. I was unhealthy, exhausted, and overwhelmed. I was overweight and wore clothes and makeup to cover up my discomfort when necessary, depending on the event or activity. I couldn't be the vibrant, lively Lisa all of the time, nor could I be the dedicated mom, parent advocate, and loving wife Maria, either. Lastly, I couldn't be the career-focused juggernaut like Alex all of the time. Each of them had a secret – and it was miserable to live a lie. The secret was that they didn't really exist. I had created them to fit each situation, to meet my needs and the expectations I placed on each role.

Going from the boardroom to a PTA meeting to some random dance club, I was moving so fast, nothing and no one could catch me. Or so I thought. It all came crashing down when my husband confronted me about a "friend" of mine I had brazenly introduced to him. I sat there, unable to look him in the eye. Life choice right there: do I keep living this lie of a life or do I tell the truth for the first time in years? Shaking and staring at the couch, I admitted it. My whole world came crashing down as the house of cards and my imaginary fairyland evaporated. I looked around and finally saw that everything was in pieces. It was like waking up in a nightmare of a world that I never knew existed behind my veil of lies. My home was a mess, husband heartbroken, and our kids were unsupported in this gray and broken world. I created a world where I was nothing, not even to myself.

I had to turn things around. For a while, I thought my situation was hopeless as I cried all of the time and wouldn't go out. Then I recalled a phrase I had heard once: *What do you do when you find yourself in a hole? Stop digging.* So I stopped digging deeper into depression and despair. I decided to get real, to become genuine with everyone in my life. Step one was being completely honest, starting with my husband. I had to face the fact that I hadn't cared about his feelings at the time. I completely ignored the fact that I loved him with all of my heart. I let anger, resentment, ongoing exhaustion, and all negative things that I created cloud the love, respect, and admiration I have for the love of my life and father of my children. This was the most painful experience of my life and I still have to live with the consequences of those choices and face them often. I wish I could go back in time, but I know that isn't possible.

The next step to turning my life around was to be honest with my family, close friends, and coworkers. I was surprised by their reactions. Some were happy that I finally admitted that I was overwhelmed and unhappy. They knew that there was more to my story than I was sharing. Then there were others who were completely shocked, who believed and trusted me all along. I broke hearts, ended friendships, lost trust and relationships that were dear to me. The pain I caused them all was heartbreaking and sad because I had no idea that my choices would affect anyone else. There were those who judged my situation but there were others who were full of love and support.

Finally, I had to be honest with myself – who was I, really? It wasn't pretty, yet it wasn't terrible. I had done some terrible things, but at my core, I was not a terrible person. I somehow got the idea that I had to strike first to stay safe, that I had to take care of my needs no matter what the cost to anyone else. I thought the world was a dark place filled with cold people and my actions, from that mental place, created a world where what I did and who I hurt didn't really matter. They weren't real! What took the longest to be honest about was that I was an alcoholic and compulsive overeater. Drinking and binge eating allowed me to stay disconnected and avoid facing the reality of my pain from living separate lives. I used them for courage when I was afraid, comfort when I was nervous, and to black out when my mind was racing so much I couldn't sleep. I had to be honest with myself and others by admitting that my addictions were dangerously unhealthy and that I needed to make a change in how I treated my body and dealt with my issues.

While I spent all my time creating and living these imaginary personas by drinking, eating, and running away from my problems, I lost track of who I used to be. There was a time when I had a deeply personal connection with God and the people around me. I had a peace about me that could make a difference with others. I remember being told I had soothing eyes and a beautiful, loving way of talking with people. I saw beauty and grace in everyone and everything that helped me live with gratitude and wonder every day. Growing up, I loved the experience of being part of a faith community and felt connected to church and my faith. I lost my faith in my late teens, early twenties and let go of what was so dear to me. My excuse was a reaction to the examples of "righteous" people in my life who let me down. When I chose those examples as the reason to change my love for my faith and connection with spirit, I lost a deep connection to who I really was. My grounded connection to God was lost. In an attempt to regain it, I now realize that I created Lisa, Maria, and Alex to try to fill the void. Through them I tried finding power in other places. I always thought I wanted to be the boss, the moneymaker or top dog, the mother and lover, as well as the independent woman. Knowing this was just the beginning of my story helped me consider what was next for me. My life didn't have to end there. I could improve my story. I could love all of me!

I had to come to terms with the reality of the situation I had created to own my part in it all. Facing who I was and who I wanted to be in real-time forced me to ask some targeted questions: What do I want? What matters most to me? I let go of my preconceptions of everything from my marriage and family to my relationships and my work. After all of the heartbreak and loss, I realized how important my spirituality was to me. I no longer need to be great at everything. I understand now that there is more room for failure, mistakes, and my own humanity. "Having it all" used to mean having a bunch of stuff such as money, power, a house, car, and anything else that made me feel important. Now, having it all for me means peace, time, acceptance, love, and joy. What I wanted was to connect with my husband, to be happy raising our children, and to enjoy doing meaningful work. I had to get in touch with my faith, God, humanity, and myself. I reconnected with my faith by seeing the good found in all people.

Getting connected with who I am and what I want has afforded me the choice of how I wanted to live the rest of my life. What will I choose? Every day offers a choice. The actions I took at that time were to cut out everything that didn't work. I burned my world to the ground, sold the properties, let go of the business, had real discussions with school administrators, and got my children the assessments and tools they needed to be successful. I gave notice at work that I would no longer travel and would cut down my hours. I sought forgiveness from those I hurt and I hired an inspiring life coach. I found a therapist and began working a twelve-step program. I stopped trying to do everything on my own and connected with friends and family.

My husband and I separated for some time. At first, I fought it, hoping the fact that I was sorry would be good enough to be forgiven. But after so much betrayal and heartbreak, it was what it was. I let go of trying to control his feelings and respected his right to choose his own path. I always loved him, yet I lied and broke his trust. That trust is something I will never get back the same as it was before; the scars run too deep to ever fully heal. We both used that time apart to learn about ourselves and grow. We stayed connected through the parenting of our children and assured each other they were our first priority.

Through honesty, focus, and action, things slowly turned around. It didn't happen overnight, but the hard work left room for many miracles. My life looks very different now from the inside out and is constantly still evolving. I fell in love with life again, including all of its ups and downs, twists and turns. I learned that I didn't have to save certain skills and traits for certain situations. Being a mom didn't mean I couldn't use my business negotiation skills with my children or with their teachers to create win-win situations. I don't have to hide my zest for life and beauty just because I'm a businesswoman. Happily, my husband and I reconnected, and I realized I could be fully honest, loving, and flawed *with* him. Being present and mindful wasn't just for meditation retreats; I could bring that to my friends and relationships. Letting go of trying to be all things to all people let me follow my path and take steps in faith. *It all came together by loving all of me, including the parts I didn't like or understand.* Life is nothing like I expect, but everything I need it to be, even when I don't know exactly what I need at any given time. I am kinder to others and myself now, giving more space for everyone to be authentic and appreciating who they are. I am accepting and can now say that I truly love all of me.

Activation Steps

What is your story so far? Remember it is just "so far." Is it what you want? Let's look at the path I took to get out of the nightmare and into reality and flow of life. You can rewrite or improve your story, too.

Step 1: **REALITY CHECK – Who am I?**

Get really honest with yourself. Who are you in different situations? Try to be honest with your personal feedback, journaling, and reflections. Be really clear about all the good, bad, ugly, and magnificent. No one need ever read your writing, so be honest with this personal inventory. Do you play lots of roles? For each role you play in your life, is it clear "who" you are? What's consistent, if anything, between them? Which characteristics will you choose to embrace? Are there qualities about you that are worth keeping? Are you stuck and can't get out? Do you need help?

Step 2: **FOCUS – What do I want?**

What really matters to you? Why do you wake up every day? Who matters most in your life? Who is worth it to you? Who do you love, honor, and want to see happy (please be sure to include YOU on the list!)? Make a clear list of what is most important to you. Let the rest go.

Step 3: **ACTION – What will I choose to do?**

What do you want? Who do you really want to be? Set some clear goals for the next three months, the next six months, and the next twelve months. Work every day to move one of these goals forward. Set at least one "cleanup goal" that will lead to forgiveness and one visionary goal that leads to an accomplishment. Wake up each morning with gratitude for the chance to make things better. Select how you will act in alignment with who you are and where you want to be. Some days it will include a five-minute activity, other days will turn into a whole-day event. It will vary in length and intensity but that's okay; the point is to create daily habits.

This is a lifelong journey of improvement and discovery. Over time, after repeating this process multiple times, you will start seeing a difference in yourself and in your relationships. This is a learning process similar to riding a bike. When you start out riding a bike on your own, it is wobbly, scary, and sometimes you fall. It's okay! You are learning, so be kind to yourself! In the early stages, it helps to have someone holding the bike, so hire a coach or get an accountability buddy. Once you get moving, figure out what works best for you whether it is journaling, reflecting, praying, meeting with a group… it doesn't matter. What matters most is that you keep pedaling! If you stop or fall over, so what? Get back up. Keep moving, keep adjusting, and stay aware and focused on your goals. My husband always says that the world laughs at you when you fall down, but it applauds when you stand back up. Who you were isn't as important as who you will become. Congratulations on your journey of improvement and discovery. It is worth it not only for you but also for your loved ones. You are making a difference for all of us. It's time you loved *all* of you, and I wish you love and blessings on this journey to self-discovery.

Luz Flores Lee

Caged Bird
Going From Soldier to CEO

I am going through a transition from being a soldier of over twenty years to a fulltime entrepreneur, which is not easy for me. As I step out in faith and boldly proclaim what God has for me, I pray my story encourages and motivates you to move forward with confidence with the vision God has placed inside of you. As Lucinda Cross would say, *"activate your life today!"*

Does getting your business off the ground seem difficult to you?

Do you struggle to hold onto your dreams and wonder if you are pleasing God?

Do you have a desire to serve others?

Do you want to give back?

You are not alone; many business owners wrestle with these questions and fear falling short of their expectations. There were many times I struggled with the same. I did not have money to pay my rent, and there were times when food was low and bills were due. At the very young age of seventeen, I had my oldest daughter, Darkema. I faced many challenges in life, including the fact that while I was pregnant with her, her father got incarcerated and was sentenced to twenty-seven years to life.

This forced me to really grow up fast. Not only was I a single mother, but I was also in need of an education. My daughter was my inspiration; I knew I had to make things better for her, so I decided to go back to school and enrolled in a GED program. I had missed so much school since I dropped out in the seventh grade; I hadn't even gone to middle school, let alone high school. And now I was enrolled in a GED program. At first it was overwhelming. I felt so lost. I took math and algebra and so many subjects I had never even heard of, like literature. I knew I needed this though, so I had to focus and study more than probably most of the group. After all, I was a mother now. There was no time for crying and quitting.

I thank God for the GED program because it gave me a different look at education. I don't know if it was the adult learning center theory that motivated me, but I started to look at education in a whole new way. I enjoyed learning. I started to thirst for more. I received my GED in four months. I can still remember that wonderful feeling. I was so proud—after all, I could now tell my daughter that I graduated from high school.

That was just the beginning of my adult life, which had started out really rocky. I met a soldier at the bus station in D.C. who I will never forget. Later, this young man turned out to be my husband. He was nice-looking and had just joined the Army.

We started dating and it wasn't long before this young man asked me to be his wife. I thought things were starting to look up for me. I was so excited, and my mother approved. We had a small wedding at my parents' house with just friends and family. I remember his mom and my mom talking about how they were so glad that we found each other.

I thought that it was a dream coming true. Since I met a man who was in the military, that meant my daughter and I would get to travel. Well, that didn't last long. My husband was abusive.

At first he started with verbal abuse, but before you knew it, he was beating me with his fists. I remember the last incident. He was yelling and cursing at me. I had my daughter in my arms, and suddenly he punched me so hard I fell into the wall, leaving both eyes black. I had become a victim of domestic violence. It was not easy being a domestic abuse survivor. There were times I thought maybe I had done something to provoke him, but it was his struggle and had nothing to do with me. I was trying to be the best wife I could be, but he did not appreciate me, so it was time for me to move on. This was in 1983.

I left my husband, moved in with family, and continued to work odd jobs here and there. My dad passed away in 1985 and my youngest sister Alicia and I applied for Section Eight, a county subsidy program that helps low-income people find a place to live. We stood in the long line all night camped out at the school waiting to put our names on a list for housing. When we got back home from my father's funeral, we had our Section Eight certificates in the mail.

That started a whole new chapter in my life. My sister and I started dating two brothers, and through this relationship, my youngest daughter Takia was born. I now had two children with no real job or career in mind. I guess you can say I sort of drifted for the next nine years, from job to job and place to place, trying to find myself.

Then one day in 1994, I decided to enlist for the D.C. Army National Guard. After all, I was older and needed a career. I called a recruiter and talked to him on the phone. He told me to make an appointment to come and see him. I did and he told me I would not have to go back to Basic Training since I completed that already. I could join but I would have to do it soon, since I would not be allowed to come back after I turned thirty-five. I had two daughters and a family and I wanted to be able to enjoy the fruits of my labor.

In March of 1994, I enlisted in the National Guard. It was during my time serving there that I was bitten by the entrepreneurial bug. I was the Deputy Commanding General's Executive Assistant, and my duties included planning and coordinating luncheons, briefings, retirements, and promotional ceremonies.

I have also used my talents to negotiate contracts and work with vendors. Later, I planned my best friend's wedding in four months, and from then on, I have been known as a wedding and event planner by family and friends. This inspired me to enroll in the Wedding and Event Professional Course with the U.S. Career Institute, where I graduated with honors. I am also certified in floral design, event planning, and interior decorating.

I have been planning events for over fifteen years now, and I will be retiring from the D.C. National Guard soon. After working for the Command Group at the Armory, I realized I had the knowledge and the expertise required to create fabulous celebrations and spectacular settings that complemented the love of friends and family at birthdays, retirements, anniversaries and weddings. I coordinated so many events successfully; I had to ask myself, why didn't I do it for money? I asked myself how much of a difference was I making in my position? Then I imagined the legacy I could leave to my daughters and grandchildren if I chose to become a business owner.

In 2007, Anointed Affairs was born. As the owner of Anointed Affairs, I have the opportunity to be an employer and make a difference in the lives of the clients I serve. I also have the opportunity to contribute to needy charities. I am looking forward to being able to fund my own charitable foundation.

Many times I have heard people say, "You're talented; you should start a business!" My family and friends know that I'm the planner and organizer among them; I see and envision the whole picture.

It is a lot of fun doing something you really like. Doing something you love makes you a natural at what you are doing.

I was ready to step into my destiny after twenty years in the military. I really could do what I had always wanted to do. I was ready for a positive change from my current position!

I had been feeling trapped and needed a way out. I love to create magic, and I enjoy helping others in a positive environment. Now I can share in the experience of couples celebrating those precious moments and happy family events. Besides, in the uncertain times that this country has faced over the last few years, people need family connection and observances.

I *am* loyal to my family and friends. I am divorced and a mother of two lovely young ladies, Darkema and Kia, and I am the grandmother of seven adorable grandchildren: Tyquan, Kemonte, Khyeema, Davonte, Khalil, Terrence and Kamille.

My passion is events. At Anointed Affairs, it is our passion to plan, organize, and create events from initial concept to finished product. We coordinate and arrange all aspects of an event as well as provide day-of direction and implementation.

As a business owner, I can leave you with a few tips that have blessed my business beyond measure. I trust that God placed the idea of this business inside of me a long time ago, and that the things I am birthing were all a part of His plan. I know that if we trust Him, He will provide.

Do not be afraid. Fear is a stumbling block that will raise its ugly head many times. Please understand that our God is unmovable and unshakable with faith. You can conquer it all. I too felt fear when seeking to leave my full-time position in the D.C. National Guard after twenty-two years of service. However, I know I must trust my Father, for He is taking me to the next level. I too have had that feeling like I wasn't adequate enough. That feeling came over me just the other day when I decided to do a number of things including launching a series of seminars and hosting a weekend retreat for aspiring entrepreneurs in August and November of next year.

I haven't had that lost feeling in a while, but that's not because I've "got it all figured out." In fact, every day I learn that there is SO much I don't know about a lot of things.

I simply hadn't felt that feeling of "OMG, I'm nervous and borderline scared" because I have been operating outside of my comfort zone for a while and now I am comfortable inside that new zone. Let me break it down like this:

Author Jamaica Kincaid said in the recent issue of O Magazine, *"People don't make changes because things are wonderful."*

We are forced to change either because something horrible happens that forces us to change or we realize that surviving in the old way of living or thinking may be safe but is way more dangerous than the new way of living and thinking. In other words, when you expand your knowledge and insight, you realize you MUST do better and push yourself, because staying the same becomes like death.

For me, this was about my 2014 declaration and commitment to embracing more love and connection with people and learning to ask for help and say "yes" when opportunities come my way.

I wasn't 100% prepared for the reality that by embracing this, I'd be forced to step into new ways of operating and thinking. I realized I had to hold myself accountable for the "new me" I said I wanted to become this year.

TRULY challenge yourself to change where you know you need to change.

I know changing is painful and that we will have to confront a whole lot of issues we really don't want to face. We have to be vulnerable on incredibly uncomfortable levels and we have to show others "I don't have it all together," but guess what? When you do this, you no longer have to hide behind anything. Your insecurities become your strength.

Remember:

New growth has to push past old pain. It's difficult, but worth it.

You must stay committed to your happiness.

Go forth and achieve the life that you have envisioned.

Share your faith because you must realize you have a mission.

We look at the calling of a Christian, to die to ourselves and take up the cross, as something we should do… if we have time. We don't take our mission seriously. Or, we think that perhaps this mission was given only to a select few specialists, such as the pastor or the missionary. This is why the world hardly notices a difference between God's people and the rest of the world.

We are so preoccupied with our own well-being, our own survival or success that we blow off the mission of God. Sharing your faith will help you understand your mission.

Perhaps that passion would so fill our souls that it would leak out into every single sphere of lives, including in our family homes and business; thus, the good news would be less of a canned pitch and more of a lifestyle. The gospel is good news, after all.

Activation Steps

1. Pray and pray often.

Prayer helps you to stay focused. It quiets your mind and allows you to hear divine inspiration as your prayers are immediately answered. For me, prayer helps me make the "right" decisions. Not from a place of having an ego, but from a place of "how may I help others and allow them in turn to help me?" I find that when I don't make time for prayer, I struggle more, work harder, and am restless. When we pray, fear falls away. When we pray, we remind ourselves constantly what we desire. And when we pray often, we hear the answers. Therefore, I pray constantly in my business daily and multiple times per day. In fact, I have time scheduled throughout my day just like it is a client appointment, but with God. It has made ALL the difference in my life… I'm not going to lie!

2. Be Authentic.

It's important to value YOUR gifts as God made you. No one is better or worse than you are, they are just gifted differently. We are all beautiful with our individuality and gifts to share with the world. The more you turn within, the more you'll find yourself and your way and learn that your uniqueness is key. Stop worrying about your "competition." Stop getting caught up in what "they have to offer" and start appreciating yourself more.

3. Use your gifts.

What good are your gifts if you don't use them? Write down your gifts. My biggest gifts that came up when I did this same exercise are to: lead, love, and care, serve, teach, share, create, and design. I want to motivate and inspire women to live the life that they deserve. I want to continue sharing in communities of like-minded individuals who inspire others to move forward.

What can you do right now to use your gifts in the world; in both big and small ways?

4. Work with others.

There is strength in numbers. When you work with others, you're collaborating your talents and gifts to get the word out (like with a bridal show, boutique event, or other sort of affair), or working as one to plan and pull off weddings and events again and again. When we work with others, I've found that this is when magic seems to happen. Many call this a mastermind. When many minds come together like one, it's like one mastermind is created and ideas and inspiration come readily and often! Appreciate others you work with. Know that without their help, your own gifts and talents wouldn't shine as brightly. And let those you work with know this truly!

Today, I'm giving you an exercise. Ask yourself these questions:

How am I making an impact in the industry (even a local impact is huge)?

What are my gifts?

How am I using my gifts to help and serve others?

I will continue to use my gifts to empower entrepreneurs to reach greatness. It takes willpower and determination. Remember you are an eagle; continue to soar. We were all destined for greatness. Let yours shine.

Vernessa Blackwell

Contributors

Vikki Johnson

Vikki Johnson is the CEO of Authentic Living Enterprises, Inc. Vikki is a TEDx Speaker, Best Selling Author, Emmy Award winning Media Executive, Founder of Girl Talk Unplugged A Sacred Sisterhood, Associated Pastor and a Proud Mom. Her life's mission is to inspire women and girls to be great in the mirror first, then the marketplace. See more of Vikki at www.allthingsvikki.com

Luz Flores Lee

Luz Flores Lee is a Life and Leadership Coach and founder of All of You Consulting. She provides life and leadership coaching, corporate team coaching, corporate training and mentoring to her clients. Luz provides her clients with the necessary tools to accomplish their goals. Luz is a dynamic individual with a strong process focus and excellent system thinking skills who has demonstrated the capability to drive business results. She's a proven leader and facilitator that can bring cross-functional, diverse groups of people together to achieve success. She graduated from The Cooper Union in New York, N.Y. with a B.E. in Mechanical Engineering and earned an M.S. in Computer Integrated Manufacturing, with a minor in Statistics, from Rochester Institute of Technology in Rochester, N.Y. See more of Luz at www.allofyouconsulting.com

Vernessa Blackwell

Vernessa is a servant of the United States with the Army National Guard. She has a passion for planning events and in 2007 she began Anointed Affairs to provide professional wedding and event coordination services to those within the DC/MD/VA area. See more of Vernessa at www.anointedaffairs.com

Never Give Up

For nearly four years, my father was a political prisoner in a third world country. Several of those years, we were unaware of his whereabouts and believed him to be dead. Then an only child, my heart was filled with the purest joy when my mother and I found out he was being released and we awaited his return.

I can remember the day he came back. That morning, I could hardly contain myself in school as I told my friends that my father was coming home. Within an hour of his return, however, my heart plummeted from the heights of anticipation to the darkest dread. Prison had changed him.

In the tortures of his jail cell, my father had found a God of judgment and severity. The father who once lavished me with affection and compliments was now emotionally and verbally abusive. His words dripped with acid, and his constant criticism slowly wore my mother and me down.

In order to protect myself, I hardened my heart. During the nights as I lay in bed and heard him demeaning my mother, I made a personal vow to never be abused again. I became defensive and overly sensitive to any type of criticism. I became incapable of receiving love and correction because I was always afraid that I was being devalued and judged as "less than!"

The first major step in my healing came through my relationship with my best friend and God-given sister Felicia, at the age of 12 during our junior high school years. Our friendship and her family's acceptance of me as one of their own taught me what it meant to be supported and loved unconditionally. I learned to begin being vulnerable with and accountable to those I trusted and they empowered me to grow with grace and truth.

During my college years, my desperation for approval strained many of my relationships with my constant need to be right and validated. Over time, I came to realize that if I spent too much time defending myself, I would miss the lessons that could help me grow.

I met my husband Marc in my early twenties. It quickly became evident that unforgiveness and unresolved issues with my father were preventing me from moving forward. Despite having a wonderful man in my life, I couldn't accept his love or maintain healthy personal and professional relationships. My relationship with Marc taught me how to accept myself without viewing correction as rejection.

I was able to move past the pain of my past because of my commitment to pleasing God. I believed that He had a purpose and plan for me, but bitterness could quickly rob me of my blessings.

My Core Message of Activation

Never Give Up! You may know how far you've come, but you don't know how close you are. It means you don't quit until you are living your vision.

I defined and owned this message nearly three years ago when I gave birth to my miracle daughter. My husband and I battled infertility issues for over ten years on our journey to parenthood. We weathered five surgeries, procedures, and negative medical reports to become parents. It was during what would be our fifth and last round of in vitro fertilization (IVF) that our daughter was conceived. I was so close to giving up, but I got up one more time. And, I am forever grateful that I did!

Having overcome seemingly impossible obstacles, I emerged on the other side of the journey with my miracle baby, a booming business, and more impassioned than ever to serve others in making their dreams a reality! How?

Activation Steps

1. I was willing to do what I'd never done before! You must be willing to do the same.

2. I re-evaluated and revamped my surroundings of people, places, and things. This is imperative for professional growth.

3. I surrounded myself with family, friends, mentors, coaches, and consultants, who had the courage to tell me the truth and did so with grace! This also is critical for personal development.

4. I refined my brand, message, and marketing materials because your brand speaks for you before you even have a chance to speak a word. This is necessary to take your life and business to the next level.

5. I worked to attract clients who were committed to their dreams and determined to change the world with their unique voice and message—people on purpose align themselves with other people on purpose.

This next set of powerful stories will give you more tips on what you need to do and the importance of "Never Giving Up!"

Gessie Thompson
www.theartofactivation.com

When Life Throws You a Curveball... Catch It!

How many times have you told someone, "I dropped the ball on that?!" Could dropping the ball have anything to do with unexpected circumstances that arose in your life that you were totally not prepared for? Perhaps you didn't see it coming. I call those circumstances curveballs. Curveballs are the unexpected things that occur in our lives and can sometimes come to us in the form of accidents, mishaps, even tragedies.

So when life throws you a curveball, instead of trying to duck it...you can catch it!

You may be wondering how you can be prepared to catch something that you weren't even expecting. Well, this is something I've come to say: "It's not what happens to you in life; it's the way you respond to it."

Oftentimes we find ourselves wanting to have complete control over a situation, and when we're prepared for something, then we're better equipped to deal with it. Preparation would more than likely put you in control of the situation. However, I'm here to tell you that even when life throws you that curveball you weren't prepared for, you CAN catch it and you can have control.

You may not always be prepared for the curveballs that life throws in your path, but when it happens, stop and ask yourself, "is this something I can change?" If you find yourself in a space where you cannot change what is happening, acknowledge that and have peace in knowing you cannot change it. If you realize that you *CAN* affect the outcome of your current circumstance, then I say ACT! Act in the way that you would want to change the "thing" that is happening so that you can have peace within you. Being able to recognize when you've been thrown a curveball and when you *can* change things will help you navigate the unforeseen occurrences in life.

I have been thrown many curveballs in my lifetime. Like the time when I met Neal H. Moritz when I was a teenager working at J. Crew in the South Street Seaport in New York City. For those of you who are not familiar with Neal H. Moritz, he is a movie producer. At the time I met him, he was working on his first film, *Juice*, which starred an up-and-coming rapper named Tupac Shakur. I engaged him in conversation based on the Def Jam jacket he was wearing. He began telling me about the movie and asked me if I would like to be an extra in the party scene they were shooting. I was excited by the opportunity! He gave me the contact information for the shoot location, and all day I thought about the possibility of being on set with stars like Queen Latifah and Tupac. But even though I was given an opportunity that most would have jumped at, I allowed fear and doubt to overcome me, and I never called. I wasn't prepared for that curveball life had just thrown me, and I dropped the ball.

That movie producer has gone on to produce many more films since then. Many of them I have seen in the theaters, such as "I Know What You Did Last Summer," "I Am Legend" starring Will Smith, "XXX" starring Vin Diesel, "21 Jump Street," and "The Fast and Furious" series, and that is just to name a few. Vin Diesel! I couldn't believe I dropped the ball on that possibility, that single opportunity that I allowed to pass me by. I am a frequent moviegoer. And when I go to the movies, I normally watch the credits roll after a movie ends. Do you have any idea the feeling I get in my stomach when I see Neal H. Moritz' name in the credits? Who knows? I could have gone on to have a great acting career based on of that single opportunity. I cannot change what I did in the past, but looking forward , if I am given that same opportunity again I will not let fear grip me; I will take ACTION!

I always wanted to be a lawyer, but instead I was talked into becoming a police officer while I pursued my law degree. Once I became a cop, my aspirations for becoming a lawyer subsided and I began focusing on rising through the ranks of the NYPD. During my twelve-and-a-half year career with the New York City Police Department, I made several arrests, mediated hundreds of disputes, endured the tragic events of the 9/11 World Trade Center attack while studying for the sergeant promotional exam, and in my tenth year, I was promoted to Police Sergeant with the NYPD. While I was still working, I began thinking about writing a book. I've always had a penchant for words and began thinking of different ideas to write about. It didn't take me long to realize what I should write about. And while I had an idea of what I wanted to write, my career with the NYPD was very demanding and as a single mother, didn't seem to have much time to write. My daughter Shelby was a tween (pre-teen) at the time and she would become the inspiration for my first book, *TOTM! Time Of The Month!® The Essential Calendar Planner for Women and Girls of All Ages*. As luck would have it, life threw me a curveball in the form of a line of duty injury that allowed me to retire.

I look at hardships as blessings in disguise. Again, it's not about what happens to you in life; it's about how you respond to it. While I had aspirations to continue climbing the managerial ladder in the NYPD, rising through the ranks, I saw an opportunity to now concentrate on my writing. I was truly blessed by my experience in law enforcement. After I retired, I began my journey into entrepreneurship. I didn't want to sit on my laurels, so I began helping my significant other, Schmoll, with his real estate business. We later became partners and had some successes. Real estate has always been a passion for my now husband and I eventually took a back seat in the real estate business. My passion was to begin a movement to empower females about menstrual wellness and I decided to begin concentrating on writing *TOTM!*.

TOTM! was created out of my need to be able to communicate with my daughter about having her first menstrual cycle. I decided to compose a book for her to track her feelings and symptoms during her monthly menstrual cycle. I also wanted to impart her with healthy tips and advice on how to deal with her period on a monthly basis. What started out as a guide exclusively for my daughter turned into a calendar planner series for girls and women to track their monthly menstrual cycles. I then began doing *TOTM!* workshops to give girls the information needed to better face their cycles on a monthly basis, including tips for how to have a less painful period.

While building my *TOTM!* business, I also began building a home-based technology business with a pretty well-known multilevel marketing company. This was a way for me to help others create an additional stream of income and seek financial freedom. So I was helping women with their menstrual problems and I was helping women and men build their own businesses.

In addition to working my businesses, I also sat on and currently still sit on the board of Brooklyn CARES Mentoring Movement. Susan Taylor, Editor-in-Chief Emeritus of Essence Magazine, began the National CARES Mentoring Movement several years ago, and today I serve as the secretary for the Brooklyn Chapter.

So there I was, serving on the board of a mentoring organization, working as a menstrual cycle maven, building a successful MLM business, and even hosting a BlogTalk Radio show for *TOTM!*. The show I presented on was called TOTM! Tea Talk, geared for women to candidly speak about that time of the month, and it aired twice a week, Wednesdays and Sundays on the internet. I did that for almost three years.

Here Comes The Curve Ball

On Thursday October 3, 2013, I was thrown one of the BIGGEST and HARDEST curveballs imaginable in my life! This time, life's curveball came in the form of loss and tragedy. Never in my wildest imagination would I or could I have fathomed the events that would unfold on that fateful day.

October 3rd was truly a game-changer for me. My seemingly perfect world was about to be shattered. Prior to that day, I was a budding entrepreneur. I was hosting my own talk show on Blogtalk radio. I was empowering women in the realm of menstrual wellness. I was civically involved. However, nothing could prepare me for what was to happen next and life as I knew it would never be the same.

It was a Thursday and I was preparing myself to go host an event for a girlfriend. She was launching her guided meditation

CD *The Voices of Zen* at the Bedford Stuyvesant YMCA and I was hosting the event! As I prepared, my phone began to ring several times in a row from unknown numbers. I finally called one of the numbers back because it had a Connecticut area code, thinking it was my sister Miriam who had called me. But it wasn't my sister; instead, it was a reporter telling me he was following up on a story that my sister was involved in. Immediately, a pit formed in my stomach. My instincts screamed to me that this was not good. The reporter began describing the car my sister drove and wanted me to confirm it. I asked him what exactly he was trying to tell me, and the reporter said, "Apparently you have not been watching TV. Turn your TV on to CNN." He was right. I had not turned on my television all day. I was, however, on my computer, and even so, I still didn't look at any of the news updates online. Even though I vaguely recalled a caption of a car chase in Washington, D.C., I hadn't clicked on it. I was too concentrated on the event that I was to host that evening.

I still had the reporter on the phone as I turned the TV on to CNN. My heart sank as I saw footage of my niece being held by an officer. At this time, I told the reporter I would call him back because I needed to process this. I needed to know what was going on. My mother then called me but I didn't speak to her. At this point, I was being handled as if I were a raw egg that my husband didn't want to drop. He spoke to my mom on the phone and said he didn't want me on the computer or watching TV. I don't think he knew what my reaction would be and was doing his best to keep me calm. He doesn't like to see to see me cry, and sometimes all we want to do as loved ones is protect those closest to us. But he was not able to shield me from the tragic news of the events that occurred that day. Reporters were now outside my house with lights flashing. They stayed camped out there all night. Life was interrupted.

I would later learn that my sister Miriam Carey was killed in Washington, D.C. by the U.S. Secret Service and U.S. Capitol Police. She was shot five times, with all shots fired from behind and striking her in her arm, back, and one in the back of her head.

At the time, we didn't know all this. All we knew was that my sister was "possibly" involved in a car chase that ended with the occupant of the vehicle being shot and killed. While the news was reporting her name on television, my family was still not properly notified of my sister's death. This prompted my sister Amy and me to drive down to Washington, D.C. the very next morning to identify the body of the person in the black Infiniti. While we were on the road in shock and disbelief at how all this was unfolding, I still had hopes that it wouldn't be Miriam lying in the morgue.

There of course are more details to this story, but I will withhold them for now. What I will say is that my sister Miriam Carey was not what the mainstream media tried to depict her as in their initial reports. While the mainstream media reported my sister as initially being a "shooter," ramming or "trying to ram the White House gate," "delusional," "schizophrenic," or "bipolar," she was **NONE** of those things. When the media realized they got the story wrong, they backed off without retracting their previous accounts. The mainstream media did not take the same zeal in reporting the autopsy report that showed my sister was shot multiple times in the back with one of the shots hitting her in the center of the back of her head. It sounded like an execution to me.

My sister Miriam was unarmed.

She was a mother, a sister, a daughter, and a friend.

She was a law-abiding citizen who was never arrested in her life.

She did not have any drugs of any kind, prescription or otherwise, in her system at the time of her death.

She did not ram or try to ram the White House gate.

She had my thirteen-month-old niece with her in the car when she was shot. It was *ONLY* by the grace of God that my niece was not shot and survived the barrage of bullets that riddled my sister's two-door Infiniti coupe. My sister was killed unjustifiably and now the agencies involved are stonewalling my family and the American people by not making the official findings public.

What I have done is began the campaign "You Plus 1." I began asking the public to write to their elected officials urging them to make an inquiry into the investigation of the death of Miriam Carey that occurred on October 3, 2013.

When my sister was killed, something in me died as well. I cannot change what has happened to my sister, but I can choose how I will respond it. I am dedicated to seeking justice for an act that was unjust. And while I mourn and cry and miss my sister, I know that she would want me to continue serving people through my volunteerism, coaching, and community activism. I'm now activating for my sister Miriam.

Opportunities

Don't drop the ball on opportunities wishing you could have, should have, or would have done something differently. I remember the late great Jim Rohn saying, "Pictures don't forget; pictures tell a story; a picture is worth a thousand words so capture the moment, click, click, done." The last time I saw my sister Miriam it was at my daughter's second annual STC Fashion Show. I had an opportunity to take a photo with her and I didn't. For no particular reason, I just didn't grab her to take the photo, even though I did take a photo with my other sister, Amy. Several days later, I texted Miriam the photo I had taken with Amy and my daughter Shelby and told her, "We didn't get to take a photo! ☹" In my mind I was saying "next time." But next time will never come for Miriam and me. That was the last time I saw my sister alive, one month and one week before her tragic death. I did, however, get some photos from the fashion show with Miriam in the background. But no pictures were taken that day of us both or of the three of us sisters all together, as we often do. Do I regret not taking the photo with her? No. Am I saddened that I didn't take the photo with Miriam? Yes. Regret weighs tons. Have no regrets in life because life is fleeting.

Do not allow your fears and doubts or excuses of not being prepared for an opportunity cost you the opportunity of a lifetime. I remember when I was presented with the opportunity to become a New York City Police Officer. I was first introduced to the opportunity when I was seventeen years old. I initially wanted to be a lawyer, but was persuaded by two officers that looked like me to take the test to become a New York City Police Officer. I didn't let the fact that I was only seventeen years old deter me from taking the test when I knew I wouldn't be eligible to be hired until I was at least twenty years old. I took the test the day before my eighteenth birthday, and I passed it with high scores. I was in the first group called. Because of my age, however, they would put my application on hold until I came of age. After an investigated thorough background check, I was sworn into the NYPD Police Academy when I was twenty-one years old. Had I not taken the test, I wouldn't have been able to then become a NYPD Sergeant and impact the lives I encountered during my career.

Disappointments And Loss

It begins with knowing what is in your realm of possibilities. What do you have control over? For starters, you have control over you! You can control whether you will cry over spilled milk or if you will simply clean up the milk that was spilled and either replace the milk or do without it. If you choose to cry over the spilled milk, you can control how long you will cry. It all begins with you!

During the tragic time that I was mourning the loss of my sister (and I'm still mourning), my multilevel marketing business took a hit. Another curveball. Had this happened at any other time in my life, I would have reacted differently. But since it happened during a time when I was dazed with grief, the business meant nothing to me. I simply didn't care. Financially, I didn't **NEED** the business. I did the business because it was a new challenge for me and at the same time I could help others to possibly retire from their current job positions.

The team I was building in my multilevel marketing business fell apart at the lowest point in my life. I lost the position I had obtained because business partners decided to quit investing in the business. A month after my sister's death, one of my business partners began trying to cross-recruit within my organization to get my partners signed up with another company. It reminded me of another cliché: "Don't kick a man when he's down." Apparently, this person didn't get that memo. What it did show me was the character of this person. The late and great Maya Angelou once said, "When someone shows you who they are, believe them the first time." What that individual showed me was that she was not trustworthy of being in my circle.

Always remember, it's not about what happens to you in life; it's about how you to respond to it.

Activation Steps

1. When opportunity knocks, open the door and receive it.
2. Don't allow your fears and doubts to knock you out of something that could be wonderful.
3. Learn to "Act" on your instincts.
4. When tragedy strikes, allow yourself time to heal. There is truth in the phrase, "time heals all wounds," but while in your healing process, don't lose yourself.
5. Take care of you and continue your life's purpose. LIVE!
6. When faced with disappointments, recognize what let you down and pick yourself back up. KEEP MOVING!

And remember, when life throws you a curveball… catch it!

Valarie Carey

Earth, Wind and Fire
Surviving The Storm Adversity

When the pain became unbearable and I started to see the holes in my superwoman cape; when my world buckled and brought me down on my knees asking, begging God to please bring me out of this nightmare that had become my life; when my marriage dissolved, when my home went from a joint, two-parent household to a single-parent household, of which I am now the head; when the debt was stacked higher than I could see and the income was less than my family's needs demanded; when I felt the depths of loneliness; when I lost my home and my cars and was about to lose my mind, that was the point where I finally reached out my hands and cried for God's help in a way I had never done before.

Here I was in the midst of the chaos that I called my life and I didn't know what to do. The problems were piling up and I felt like I was taking one hit after the other. I was drowning in despair and hopelessness. I needed to see my way through what I call the storm of adversity. I needed God's guidance and a way out.

Where do I go From Here?

My life was beyond a mess and somewhere in my heart I knew that God was working on me but I didn't understand why everything that was so near to me had to tumble down at one time. I'd been through challenges in my life before but nothing like this. I didn't know where my life was heading but I did know that I'd been victorious over past challenges. Since I was victorious in the past, I already had a road map to help me through the current dark times. I began to apply what I learned about God's transformative power, empowerment tools, and my own life experiences. I called on those same foundational tools, laws, and principles that I used to transform from an incest victim to a survivor; to go from a generational welfare participant to Welfare to Work Trainer and Case Manager and beyond; to change my view of myself from a woman of low self-worth to a woman of great self-worth, self-esteem and confidence. These tools became the steps of the power program that helped me to keep thriving after divorce, to increase my income tremendously, to find a new home for me and my children, and to love myself through it all. The first step in this power program I'm sharing with you here is to:

Get Still

In order to see past the storm of divorce, the decrease in pay, becoming a newly single parent and losing my home, I had to get still. Getting still meant that I had to quiet my mind, clear my heart, and connect with the power within me. However, with the overwhelming feeling of being abandoned by my children's father, knowing that I was now the sole provider living with the paralyzing fear that I wouldn't be able to provide, and dealing with so much hurt and loneliness that I was nearly driven to suicide, getting still seemed almost impossible. It became even more impossible because of the distractions I allowed in my life to keep me from facing my issues which felt too painful for me to address. I used the company of the television to comfort me, I used sex to release the stress, and I needed to be around people to distract me from what I was feeling. I was always looking for an escape from the pressure of the responsibility I was left with. My mind was constantly filled with fear about my survival and how I was going to literally clothe, feed, and provide shelter for my children.

One thing that I've learned in my life (but sometimes choose to forget) is that we always have what we need. In this moment, meditation was my doorway to the stillness and peace that I needed to experience. I've been taught by masters, practiced it regularly, and taught the principles and application of meditation to others for years, so I innately knew how important it was for me to meditate. Getting still required me to clear my mind and surrender every meaning I gave to my current situation, including judgment of myself and being a hurt, lost, lonely and confused victim. Meditation was the key to my surrender.

However, despite what I had learned and experienced through meditation, I still allowed my fear and distractions to grow so strong that I abandoned my meditation practices. When I made the choice to begin meditating again, I started with two to three minutes at a time, and then my mind was back on guard duty. My meditative moments then expanded to five and then ten minutes at a time. Soon after, I had mornings that I could meditate for twenty minutes at a time, learning moment by moment to get still and draw close to God. Once I was still, I was able to listen for guidance. I could feel the love and comfort all around me and I found reasons to be grateful. Getting still enabled me to trust life and to trust my intuition again. It also gave way to forgiveness and through the powers of love and forgiveness I am able to heal my heart. Getting still opened the gateway to the wisdom, energy, and discernment I needed to begin rebuilding my life.

Getting Focused on What's Important to You

Can you imagine getting so focused on what you desire to experience that you are able to manifest it? Sometimes it feels like that's easier said than done. During my adversities and struggles I couldn't focus on anything but the problems I was experiencing.

During this time, I couldn't afford the home we were living in. I was about two months behind on my payments and couldn't see myself getting any closer to reconciliation. My pay was about to be cut and I had four children to care for. I had no idea how I would find the energy or mental wherewithal to spend additional time making extra money. I was at a loss. My plan was to move in with my mother in Baltimore and commute to Prince George's County and the Washington, D.C. area daily to get the children to school and myself to work. However, I did not have a car so I planned a way to travel by public transportation. We were all set to go when my great aunt came to visit and asked if we wanted to stay with her. My aunt lived in Prince George's County and although my sons and I would have to share a bedroom, she promised to help make it work. I was elated and extremely grateful.

However, soon after moving in, I became depressed. I judged myself harshly and focused on my hardship. As an adult, I never had to depend on anyone to that extent. I felt like a failure and focused on what a bad mom I was and how terribly I had let my children down. I lost sight of the blessings in my life. I lost sight of all of the great people that were around to support me. All I saw was how far off track I was from my goals and the fact that I was sharing one bedroom with my three sons.

I couldn't grasp the reality of what was becoming of my life. I felt trapped, so I made a choice to get laser-focused on the life I desired to live and the person I desired to be. My negative mental and emotional focus had been dominant in my being. Changing this mentality took time and it took work. I first began to talk out loud to myself. This was important because it helped my "power thoughts" build strength and resonance within me. Soon my power thoughts were louder and stronger than my negative ones. I then began to feel happier, more excited, enthusiastic, and grateful for my life. As I built my mental and emotional stamina, I was more receptive to the vision that God had for me to play out in my mind. Daily, I began to see a new me and a new life and that became my focus. I turned my attention to my vision and practiced sharpening it. Even if it were only pieces at a time, I sharpened the picture in my mind by focusing on it.

With time, I began to add emotion to the vision and my vision began to take on a life of its own. What once seemed dim was now bright with hope.

I share this to demonstrate that even when you feel at your lowest, there is always a glimpse of light for you to identify and focus on. Once you get focused, you will…

Become the Essence of What you Want to Experience

Mahatma Gandhi said, "*Be the change* that you wish to see in the world." It was up to me to determine how I was going to be the change I wanted to see in my world. I wanted a new home, an increase in pay, security for myself and my children, and a loving relationship. In order for this change to occur and the transformation to take root, I had to become the love, safety, comfort, and security that I wanted to experience in my relationships. I became and am still becoming the essence of the healthy relationship I wanted in my life. To experience these qualities meant that I had to become the qualities. I began to love myself more deeply by taking time to appreciate everything about me, to speak sweetly to myself, to encourage myself more and show myself the care I needed. I began practicing forgiveness regularly, to care for my needs, and to release myself from judgment for all of the mistakes I made. While I am still preparing myself emotionally and mentally for a healthy relationship, I feel increasingly confident that I will attract an amazing partner in my life.

In my career, it became important to become a living, walking symbol of value and worth. I appreciated and saw the value in everything I did well and every skill I possessed. I complimented myself on a job well done every chance I got. I gave myself high-fives when needed and I constantly fed myself positive self-talk. It became a habit to build myself up and see the value in everything that I brought to the table. And within a short period of time, I received two raises and ultimately made a career move that increased my income significantly. Not only did my income increase, but I was also in an environment where I was appreciated for all of my experience and skill sets. The environment shifted to support me as I contributed to it.

With time, patience, and consistency, huge debts were paid off and we were able to secure a new home. My sons and I excitedly moved into a place of our own fourteen months after moving in with our aunt. While those fourteen months seemed like an eternity, they allowed me the time and space needed to heal and be restored. Our new home was almost handed to me despite my financial and credit adversities. During the time we lived with my aunt, I meditated on being secure, having a loving space to live in, and I saw myself taking care of a new home. I became the essence of what a loving, healthy home is and that is exactly what I am experiencing now. The timing was perfect and we were able to move in with ease.

With the increased income, new work environment, and new way of viewing relationships, I had the energy to TURN UP MY LIFE!

Turn up Your Life!

To turn up your life means to increase the positive vibrations in your life that will keep you thriving and energetic as you move through adversarial periods in your life. The vibrations of optimism, joy, happiness, love, peace, enthusiasm, and abundance are key to helping you release the sadness, confusion, and pain you may feel when experiencing adversity. To help turn up my positive vibrations, I would greet every morning with an amazing smile and reverence for life. Even when circumstances weren't going right in my life, I found things to be grateful for. I became responsible for how I felt and how I chose to view my life, and I turned up my energy to reflect how amazing and grateful I felt. The glow in my smile was a reflection of what I was feeling inside.

Turning up the energy in my life helped me uplift others when I shared my testimony about the troubles I was going through. When I shared my story of divorce and living on poverty level even with a job, people often wouldn't believe that I was going through something so traumatic. They often voiced how inspired they were to push forward despite their worries.

I also kept my enthusiasm on high to weaken the depression that could take root at any moment. The higher I turned up my appreciation, gratitude, joy, enthusiasm, happiness, and excitement, the more amazing opportunities began to open for me and the more I was able to contribute by sharing my story. Changes began to occur in my life in ways that I can't explain. I had a new job offer with a significant pay increase, I was given the opportunity to work in a field and environment that I love, my children began to excel in school and in their personal lives, and I started meeting some really great men who supported me along the way. My best girlfriends became increasingly loving, caring, and supportive of me. I am so excited about the changes in my life and I know that you can see your way out of the current storm in your life as well. I want to share with you a few how-tos to help you survive the storm of adversity when you are in need of a "life lift."

Activation Steps

1. **Get still**—learning to meditate will be a tremendous support to you in your life. Find a practice that works for you. Whether it's a simple relaxation technique or an in-depth, soul-healing meditation practice, get still and go within.
    A. For Starters: Guided meditations are great. You can purchase audios or videos to lead you through this process.

    B. You can also start meditating in five to ten-minute intervals before you start your day.

    C. Get in a quiet space and begin to breathe in

through your nose and out through your mouth. Let your thoughts flow. No judgment; don't try to force them to be positive. Be a quiet observer. As you sit and breathe, focus on your breath. Feel it flowing in and out. Imagine yourself breathing in fresh, clean energy and breathing out stress-filled, negative energies. It's important to relax so you can meet these challenging times with grace and ease.

2. **Become the essence of what you desire**—turn your attention away from what's disturbing and hurtful. This may be difficult at first but I want you to take the time to practice dwelling on what you want to experience.

    A. Identify what you want to experience and breathe life into that vision by imagining how you would feel if you had it.

    B. Practice this daily, after or during meditation, while you are shopping, taking a walk, or just enjoying some private time and watch how powerfully you will manifest.

3. **Turn up your life**—focus on and intensify the good feelings within you.

    A. If you find yourself feeling really sad or down, talk to yourself positively (either silently or out loud).

    B. Speak life into your desires. Speak about the good in your life, the excitement that you will experience when you accomplish your goals and the good things that will come out of your desires being manifested.

C. Find the smallest things to get happy about. Look at nature and pay attention to all of the miracles of life you see there. You are conditioning yourself to find the good.

D. Embrace your current situation and begin to find the lessons in them. This will turn up your confidence and hope, giving you the energy to keep thriving.

4. **Take bold steps forward**—you have to do something with all of the love, appreciation, strength, and positive energy you've built up.

   A. Create your plan of action. Write down a step-by-step plan of how you want to move forward in your life. This step is easily missed when we are dealing with adverse circumstances because we are so focused on getting out of the pain. When you are creating your plan, be sure to factor in anyone or any circumstance that would be affected by your plans so you can be successful (i.e. your children's schedules or your budget).

   B. Find a support group, a coach, or professional help to aid you in taking the steps you need to take.

   C. Take baby steps. When moving through and out of adversities, it is often necessary to take small steps at a time.

D. Keep track of your progress. The victories are so important during this time. Your sense of accomplishment will help you to rebuild your hope and trust in yourself.

E. Move in the face of fear. When you are overwhelmed, remember that the adverse moments will pass and you have a choice to stay stuck in the same place or to create powerful changes in your life.

LaTalya Palmer

Nothing Can Come Between Us
Building Family from the Heart

As far as I can remember, I always loved and valued family. I enjoyed watching the famous family sitcoms on television such as *The Cosby Show, The Brady Bunch, Mr. Belvedere, Diff'rent Strokes,* and more. I would observe how each member of the family would interact with each other in one way or another. I watched how each member in the family handled life's challenges one day at a time. In my eyes, this is what family was all about and anything outside of this made no sense. To me, the sitcoms provided me with a glimpse of what building a family from the heart could look like. This was my reality as a child growing up. Was this your reality as well?

It was not until I was older that I realized what I was seeing on television was all staged and what I experienced in reality was completely different. What I saw in real life was a single mother—my mother—slaving long hours working through nights and never taking a vacation for herself or her children. I saw a woman serving in both parental roles and struggling through the process. I did not see a husband and a wife working in partnership to build a family. I did not see a husband mentoring his son or daughter through the developmental stages that at times can be very difficult.

Although that was a reality for some of my friends in the neighborhood, in our house it was not. Our truth at home was seeing our mother exhausted, frustrated, and rejected, yet determined to make it in spite of the struggles of single parenthood. Desperately attempting to give her children what she had growing up was a reality she would never be able to see manifest. The joys of having both parents in the home to raise the children would only be a memory she had from her childhood. To her, the cost of raising children on her own was a far greater disaster than raising them with someone else. As a result, she desperately attempted to give us this same experience for years and failed with every attempt.

As I reflect back to those seasons of my life, I can now say that I spent almost all of my childhood days suffering in silence as a result of my mother's truth. There were many struggles I did not share with my mother not because I believed she did not care, but rather because of fear, not wanting to stress her out more than she already was. Her struggles as a single parent regretfully caused her to make decisions that were not always the best. From disciplining her children to the manner in which she communicated with us, when compared to those families on the television sitcoms and those of my friends; we were a family of dysfunction in my eyes.

For years, I hid my childhood scars deep in my heart. This included rape, many failed suicide attempts, running away from home, continuous molestation, abortion, a night in jail, and many other challenges—life for me did not look promising. These scars were so deep that the sound of defeat screamed louder as the voice of hope was silenced from the chains on my heart and in my core. Though my mother did the best she could with the hand she was dealt, it did not protect me from the challenges I would one day come face-to-face with from childhood and into my adulthood journey.

What I saw on television compared to what I saw daily at home left me perplexed and bewildered as a child. As I began to really take a look at my mother's core, I realized that her definition of building a family was based on what others told her or what she saw growing up. Once I realized that, I no longer was bound by my feelings. No longer were the chains on my heart holding me from loving myself or living. That freedom allowed me to see that she did what she thought was best based on what she knew. Although it did not look like it at first, I now realize as an adult looking back that she is my hero.

Looking at my mother's life script inspired me to change mine as I looked at the core of what she was doing overall as a woman. Though I saw her struggles as a single parent, I knew deep down she was a survivor. I realized at a very young age that my mother's tenacity to survive was like no other woman's that I knew. With every failed relationship, my mom got right back up and kept on moving. She had the strength of a lion and was determined to roar as she made the best of her situation.

Not wanting to be another statistic or remain in my current reality, I decided to use that which terrified and wounded me as a child to fuel my existence as an adult. I decided to go on a voyage of discovering who I was, who I am, and who I wanted to become. This was and still is a never-ending expedition; however, I am happy to say that my life script is different from that of what I saw as a child growing up. Why? Because I decided at the age of seventeen that I would focus on building myself from within so that the future family I desired would be built from the heart instead of from what others expected or what I saw. It was then that my mind and heart became ready to understand and accept the life I had as a child. It wasn't easy, to say the least and it still is a journey, but instead of allowing it to break me, I'm using my past as a stepping stone to my future.

I decided that if I built my family from the heart, the results I experienced would be different. I am certainly not an expert on matters of the heart; however, I do know what the Word of God says. In 1 Samuel 16:7, the Lord was speaking directly to Samuel when He said, "Do not look at his appearance or at his physical stature, because I have refused him, for the Lord does not see as man sees; for man looks at the outward appearance, but the Lord looks at the heart." In another scripture, I found that in Jeremiah 17:10 (NKJV) God says, "I, the Lord, search the heart, I test the mind, even to give every man according to his ways, according to the fruit of his doings."

By searching the scriptures, I was able to redefine my reality that was embellished by television and tarnished by my life's experience. The challenges I endured during my childhood and as a part of my young adult life deprived me of some things that, at the time, I thought were lost eternally. You see, my truth caused me as a child to have anger problems, attitude problems, and more in spite of who I really was. I was never a person who hated people or was just flat-out mean. I was one that was and still is very happy and charismatic, but found it difficult to stay in that place consistently. However, something changed within me and I was determined to become the person the scriptures told me I was.

According to the scriptures, I am fearfully and wonderfully made. I was created in the image of God and I was so precious in His eyes that He sacrificed His only Son so that I may have life and have it abundantly. This fueled my ambition to live the life I deserved and craft happiness from the heart instead of from my mind. I was determined to rewrite my life script by working on those areas that left my heart stained.

This hunger, this drive pushed me to make bold moves on my journey. I began trailblazing through the memories that haunted my past to the light that was pulling me towards my future. This light was far beyond the reach of my mentality, but near enough in my radar for me to believe I could get there.

That light was the family I knew I would one day have. The children I would one day give birth to with the husband I would one day love. If for whatever reason my future life did not include a husband to help raise my children, I was still going to build my path differently. Building a family from the heart prepares and equips the parent as well as the child to live in unity as they partner with each other on this journey called life.

My vision for my life now required me to expand myself beyond my comfort zone. I could no longer hide from my past. I began sharing my story with my friends as a way of healing myself and mentoring them. This helped me to free myself from the shame that inundated my life. The more I shared, the more I became stronger and my transformation began unfolding right before my eyes. I chose to no longer dwell on the past. Though the road was filled with challenges, I was determined to live a life that would build the legacy I wanted to leave behind. In order to achieve this, I had to FOCUS on my future, my legacy, my destiny, my family, and nullify the generational shackles that desperately attempted to tarnish my future.

I put myself in situations or atmospheres that required me to network in hopes of discovering who I really was from the heart. You see, fear is what kept me silent for years. Fear is what kept my heart bound and stained with bitterness, hopelessness, anger, depression, and despair. In order for me to become free, I had to create this self-discovery path FEARLESSLY! I began connecting with people I did not know in hopes of reshaping my surroundings. I traveled far to go to high school in spite of not having the proper transportation because I was determined to rewrite my life script my way. I was intentional in taking responsibility for my decisions and never lived in regret. Staying bound or chained by fear was not an option. Allowing the "should have," "could have," or "would have" song to penetrate my mind and saturate my heart was no longer an option. I was determined to rebuild myself regardless of whether I had someone to hold my hand or not. I would do it even if I was the only one who believed in myself. Though the journey is never ending, it was worth creating the paths FEARLESSLY.

Walking fearlessly required me to remain OPTIMISTIC. Looking at the situations presented to me from an optimistic lens opened new doors that had never been open before. This made me realize that I controlled my decision to either accept or reject the options, both good and bad that were presented to me. I had the choice to remain the victim or become the victor. The expectations imposed by others no longer hindered me from discovering who I was. The many activities I intentionally put myself in by serving others in school and the community helped me discover myself while remaining fearless and optimistic. This helped me stay inspired because when life kicked me in the butt, I remembered that light that was pulling me to my future.

I then took CONTROL of my mental ship, for I was the captain. I knew time was indispensable and life itself was precious. As I took control of my life, my attitude, behavior, conversations, and mindset began to change. I realized that having a colorful language did not represent the Sindy of my future but the Sindy of my past. You see, the old Sindy had a sharp tongue and popped off on people at any given time. The new Sindy was worth discovering and remolding with the help of God. This self-control only became a reality when I gave my life to Christ. This was not an overnight process but it was easier with the help of the Holy Spirit, prayer, and reading what God said about me in His Word.

As I came to know who I was to God, I began to UNDERSTAND and accept my past better. Why? Because my past was going to be the testimony I would one day use to save other children, parents, and even the family I would have one day. Understanding my past allowed my heart to be freed from the chains of silence as I dealt with my core. This step was the most rewarding and fulfilling because I began evolving into the beautiful butterfly that I was created to become. These first three areas were key in setting me free to be me and it felt so good.

Finally, I stood tall and shined like the diamond I was. Why? Because I finally knew who I was, who I belonged to, and where I was going. No longer was I concerned with the differences that were embedded in my core. No longer was I ashamed of my trials. No longer was I concerned with what people said about me, against me, or to me. I was a child of God who was fearfully and wonderfully made. I had the power through the blood of Jesus to focus, remain optimistic, and maintain self-control while understanding my past as I used it to fuel my uniqueness to illuminate my path through the darkness of tomorrow.

You see, I had to go through this process in preparation for the family I would soon create. You may not have had to go through the exact same experience I did, but I am quite sure you have a story. A story that you know has kept you bound from experiencing the life you deserve. I am quite sure there is a family you long for as your own. I am quite sure that you have a current family that you are seeking to make things better with and are seeking ways or avenues to figure out how.

This dream or desire or longing will not come to pass if you do not deal with your past. The past that makes you sit back and soak in pity, shame, guilt, or hurt. This past that you believe may have damaged your core from ever being restored. I could not get to a place of building a family from the heart if I did not experience having one without it. As a child growing up, I could not see any light clearly, or so I believed. The only thing I had to hold onto was what I saw on television with every fiber of my mind and soul.

The ability to dream, imagine, hope, and believe that one day my life would look like *The Huxtables* was enough to ignite me. What dreams do you currently have for a family if you do not already have one? What ways can you change the current reality of your family to one that is identical to a family that was built from the heart? In order for you to build a family from the heart, you must be able to love. To love others, you must first love yourself with all of your imperfections, shortcomings, shames, guilt, past hurts and all.

Activation Steps

1. **Focus on taking time to *heal* from those wounds.**
   This is why you must first love yourself. To not love yourself is to say you do not love God, for we were created in His image and likeness. When God created you,

He used His hands to do it all. He perfectly molded you to look just like Him. He did not use a donkey or fish or the wood from the trees to create you. That alone should ignite your desire to love yourself. This is not going to happen in a day, so take time out to work on this.

2. **Focus on *embracing* your flaws, imperfections, challenges, and your past, and live again.** This will help you free yourself from your past as you embrace the possibilities of your future. The future that pulls you to live, exhale, and love. Why? Because the family you are building will be built to last.

3. **Focus on *appreciating* every single moment, whether good or bad.** The good ones give you a reason to celebrate. Celebrate every achievement, victory, and milestone of your family. Allow the bad moments to give you an opportunity to learn from the challenges, for these challenges are not meant to break you but to make you stronger.

4. **Focus on building the *relationship* of the family.** It is the relationship within a family that serves as a sealant to keeping every member united. Without this, the relationship, the core values, beliefs, and ability to love will disappear into thin air.

5. **Lastly, focus on building *trust*,** for it is through trust that forgiveness can be extended, acceptance can be experienced, and understanding can be gained.

Until you are freed of your past and your core is restored, building a family from the heart will not become a reality for you. Granted, this process is an ongoing one, but it will help you get through the hard seasons of life. Both my children were born before my husband and I were united as one under the covenant of God. As a result, challenges came as well as victories. Because I knew the results would be promising, I am determined to FOCUS on my future and joyfully take this journey in building my family from the HEART. Why? Because my future, my children's future, and my husband's future are worth the investment.

Sindy Eugene

Contributors

Gessie Thompson

Author of *Hope Beyond Fibroids: Stories of Miracle Babies and the Journey to Motherhood*, New York-based Brand Strategist and Fertility Coach Gessie Thompson helps women and men navigate the challenges they encounter to conceive or carry their visions to full term. As a Fertility Coach, she supports them to overcome the emotional and mental hurdles that accompany infertility. As a Brand Strategist, she partners with entrepreneurs to package and give "birth" to their brilliance so they are positioned to change the world with their unique voice and message. She has been featured in *ESSENCE* magazine and has appeared on "The Yolanda Adams Morning Show," "The Tom Joyner Morning Show," ARISE TV, SABC News, "On Point Talk with Carlette Christmas," and "The Frank Ski Morning Show." See more of Gessie at www.upliftgroup.com

Valarie Carey

Once featured on the cable television network LifeTime sharing the message of menstrual
wellness, Valarie Carey is a retired New York City Police Sergeant turned entrepreneur. She is the founder of TOTM! Time Of The Month!® and author of calendar series by the same name.
TOTM! Time Of The Month!® (Val's Word! Publishing) hands out tips and advice for girls and women of all ages who menstruate. Valarie Carey often called Val, conducts TOTM! menstrual wellness workshops for teens, women, and single dads. Val is a mentor and community activist in her native Brooklyn neighborhood of Bedford Stuyvesant. See more of Valarie at www.facebook.com/ValCareyNY

LaTalya Palmer

LaTalya Palmer is the Ignite Your Life Coach and Trainer with a twist of sexy and fun. LaTalya work with single moms who are ready to get unstuck, re-ignite their fire and dreams while raising their children or rising from adversity! She believes that every woman has the power they need within to rise from the ashes of life adversities, and create new beginnings from the lessons learned. As a divorcee and single mom of four, she knows what it's like to put her children first and her dreams on the back burner. LaTalya understands how easy it is to get tired of fighting and want to give up. She also knows what it is to rise from those adversities, own and manifest my dreams while raising successful children. As a certified life coach Ms. Palmer teaches single moms who have lost their mojo how to bring life back to their dreams and passions, so they can BECOME the irresistible success magnets they were created to be. As a certified Empowerment Trainer she uses interactive, focused, Skill Building and Action Oriented Facilitation to help single mothers regain confidence and belief in themselves. They are taught the personal development, professional, interpersonal and technical skills they need to stand out in a competitive world. See more of LaTalya at www.igniteyourfemininepower.com

Sindy Eugene

Sindy Eugene is the Founder and President of Global Youth Empowerment Movement, Inc. & My V.O.I.C.E Matters International. She is committed to helping parents and children around the world as she dedicates her life to motivate and educate them on how to rewrite their life's script to succeed through partnering with each other. She is known as "The Student Pathfinder" and has helped students from different walks of life get on the right path to academic and social success. She has worked with traditional and nontraditional students, military personnel, immigrant students, first-time college students, middle and high school students, high school drop outs, and business professionals seeking to further their education.

As a result of her proven results and passion for student success, colleges, universities, churches, private schools, for profit and nonprofit organizations seek her expertise on College Readiness, College Transition and Leadership Development workshops/seminars for their students, clubs and/or organizations in addition to serving as a keynote speaker. See more of Sindy at www.gyem.org

The One

Releasing my limiting beliefs and self-doubt has been the biggest (and most challenging) piece of moving forward for me. That little girl who thought she wasn't good enough has grown into a woman of faith, perseverance, and strength.

I remember my first dose of motivation from when I attended my first seminar, entitled, "The Turning Point," which was a real turning point for me. An "Aha" moment came and I realized that I did not have to work for others. I had the guts to step out on my own and create a full service title, mortgage, and real estate investment company. The key, I discovered, was in learning to think differently. I had all the business skills and training I needed but what I didn't have before that time was belief in myself. Since that time and place in 2002, I've continued make mastering my mindset the #1 priority and I do so through a daily practice of pouring into my mind with positive uplifting books and cd's, meditation and journaling and surrounding myself with like-minded and like- spirited people.

<u>My Core Message of Activation</u>

Treat each person you meet as if he or she is "The One!" Because, guess what, she is! He is! Life is about people and relationships. The more we value each other, the more we will connect at a core level, revealing how we can be of service to each other. It's not so much about meeting "The One" but instead, *being* "The One" for others. When we show up to be "The One" for others it instantly clears the path for meaningful connections. *The One Philosophy* has been my foundation for as long as I can remember. I've always believed that each person I meet was put in my path for a reason. At times it's for me to learn something, at others, it's about them learning from me.

Activation Steps

1. **Don't judge!** This applies to yourself (self-judgment) and especially to others, for we all have value on this earth.
2. **Have faith!** Know that God has greatness instilled in you and it is your responsibility to honor that.
3. **Keep yourself surrounded by people who believe in you and your dreams.** It will keep you activated.
4. **Support those who will support you and hold your vision with care.**

The next set of stories will enlighten you on the importance of good relationships and how all relationships play a part in your transformation

Nancy Matthews

Kiss of Life
Live an Abundant Life Through Service

It happens to us all. I'm not talking about wrinkles or gray hair…I'm talking about the moment that you realize that you have turned into your mother!

Now, I have always looked like my mother since before I can remember, so that's not what I'm talking about. I'm talking about the moment you say the things your mother used to say or do the things your mother used to do when you were growing up. Fortunately for me, in addition to those things, I also picked up my mother's generous spirit.

My mother is the original super volunteer! She was the person who combed every little girl's hair in the neighborhood in the morning before going to work. When other kids couldn't count on their parents, they could always count on "Aunt Betty," the name the neighborhood kids had given her – even those not related by blood. My mother was in the delivery room for many of the neighborhood babies when the parents or "baby daddies" weren't there for one reason or another. My mother did and still does drive people to the hospital, dialysis appointments, the supermarket, and even to work and she is eighty years old!

All of my life, I've heard "it is better to give than to receive." And since I've lived around that giving spirit all the years that I was growing up, it's no surprise that I picked up those traits. In giving without expectation, I've learned some great lessons over the years. My hope is that by sharing some of my stories and lessons, I can lead you to your own life lessons.

A Soda and a Smile

I was rushing to meet some friends but stopped to pick up something at a drugstore, thinking it wouldn't take very long. I was in line behind a young woman, very thin and pale with stringy brown hair. She had on short cut-off shorts and a tank top and smelled like a smoker. She had gotten a soda which she already opened and taken a few sips. I was annoyed and impatient because she was slowly counting out change to pay. She and the cashier realized that she didn't have enough money, but because she had started drinking the soda, she couldn't put it back. She began to panic, so I impatiently yelled from behind that I would pay for the soda and told her to keep her change. It was a kind act, but I definitely didn't do it in a kind way. My annoyed tone and annoyed look were obvious. She took her soda and money and went out the door while I finished paying for my purchase.

Rushing again, I left the store and jumped in my car, starting the engine. Before I could put on my seatbelt, there was a knock on my window. It was the woman with the soda and she was crying. I rolled down the window assuming she was going to ask for more money. Instead, she reached in the window, grabbed my hand and thanked me for helping her, stating that nobody had ever done anything that nice for her before. She went on to say, "I was thinking about killing myself, but decided not to because you showed me there is still kindness in the world." She then backed away from the window while continuing to look at me saying "Thank you. Thank you. Thank you." I rolled up my window, backed out of the parking space, and drove away stunned because it was only a $1.39 bottle of soda….

Lessons Learned: You never know what others are going through. A kind word, smile, or gesture could be just the thing needed to help them out of that dark place they may be in. You may be the sign from God that they were looking for.

Coworker, My Coworker

Did you ever have a coworker who always volunteered for the high-profile presentations but needed your help to complete their PowerPoint slides? A coworker who claimed she didn't know how to do any of the mundane work so you had to do it? Who offered you the work that she didn't want to do as a "developmental opportunity"? A coworker who seemed to do less work, but definitely made more money? Well, I had one of those coworkers, and this is the story of how we became friends.

The company had just gone through a huge restructuring and we both landed in new positions in the same group. When it came time for us to handle the change management from our team, she volunteered to lead the manager and supervisor meetings and suggested I lead the trainings for the customer service representatives. When we worked late, she asked me to step out and get dinner for the team, while she stayed behind and continued to work closely with our boss. And even though we were peers, she seemed to assign more work to me than my boss did. Saying I didn't like this woman was an understatement….

Then one morning she sent an email to me and about 150 others saying that she had brain, spinal fluid, bone, and bone marrow cancer. She asked us all to pray for her as she started experimental treatment. She kept working during her treatment so I got to see her lose her hair and all of the other side effects of chemotherapy. Because she also had small children, we put together a list of things we could do to help the family – bring dinners, go shopping, and eventually give her rides back and forth to treatment when she could not drive herself. The first time I drove her, we sat in the waiting room, waiting to be called back to the treatment room. When she was finally called, she asked me go back with her. The nurse escorted us back, weighed her, took the rest of her vitals and took us into a white, impersonal room to await the doctor. She sat on the gurney with her legs dangling over the side and I sat in the guest chair across from her. While waiting, we chatted about meaningless things like her favorite flowers being pink crape myrtles.

The doctor came and had her lay on her back on the gurney. He took a needle and put it in a port at the top of her head, forcing clear fluid through a tube and into her head. I listened in as the two of them talked about her treatment, not understanding most of what was being said. During that time, he also drew some fluid out for testing. He left the room and she sat up, joking about how much all of this would cost and how it would affect her rates the following year. She told me since she had already met all of the out-of-pocket maximums for the prescription drug and medical plans; she threw all of the bills away when they were sent to her, explaining that she no longer even paid the copayments for these visits. Then the doctor came back in and said that there were no cancer cells in the fluid. She looked at me and said "Oh my God," declaring that I was her good luck charm. Because she wasn't the hugging type, I just squeezed her hand and congratulated her. We both walked out of the office with tears in our eyes and had a great conversation about her future while I drove her home. She shared with me that this was her second bout with cancer; the first was while she was pregnant with her second daughter. She decided to delay treatment until after the baby was born. She also told me that she would be grateful if she could have just one more year with her family.

After that moment, we became fast friends. I was able to share with her the things she did at work that bugged me. She shared that a mentor once told her to avoid learning the mundane things because as a woman, she would get stuck doing them. I drove her to many more chemo treatments and was offended when others signed up for the driving schedule. I gathered up home-cooked dishes and money from our other coworkers, bought a basket of books for her girls, and even contacted the 100+ people she had emailed about her diagnosis to gather get well messages and compiled those into a keepsake for her to read when she was too sick to come to work. I visited her when she could still talk but nothing she said made sense. I visited her when she could no longer talk and I had to make up things to say to keep the conversation going. I also visited her when she just kept her eyes closed and we sat in silence. During that time, our coworkers would come to me first to ask me to help them prepare for taking her to chemo, or they mentioned that they were scared to take food to her house for fear that they couldn't handle seeing her. I told them all, "-You get through it by taking the attention off of yourself and putting it where it belongs…on her." Unfortunately, she passed away within a few months of this second cancer diagnosis. I had a crape myrtle tree planted in her memory outside of our office building.

Lessons Learned: Speak up when someone does something that annoys you. Who knows—once you clear the air, you might become fast friends. When serving others, take the attention off of yourself. It's not about you; it's about them.

The Blind Leading the Blind

I was volunteering as an usher for a sold-out show. My job was in the lobby, helping get everyone to the right location in the six-level, 2,500-seat theater. The lobby was extremely crowded as patrons from the previous show were pushing to get out and patrons for the next show were shoving to get in.

As I looked out over the sea of people, I saw a blind couple sharing a single white cane get out of a cab and walk towards the theater. I made my way through the crowd to the couple and asked if they wanted assistance. The man said yes and asked that I take his wife's arm and lead them to their seats. I let the lead usher know that I was leaving to escort them to their seats. I took their tickets and realized they were up on the sixth floor and my trip would not be as quick as I thought it would be.

We made it to the sixth floor and almost to their seats when the husband suggested I take them to the restroom. I led him to the men's room door and let him go in alone with the white cane. His wife did not have a cane so I walked her into the restroom and to a stall. I finally got them to their seats and asked if I could do anything else for them, expecting them to say no. I was surprised when the husband asked if I could read the Playbill to them! What? Read the Playbill? I was getting a bit anxious because I was away from my post for so long, but I complied and read the Playbill from cover to cover. As I finished, I realized that although I was a theatergoer for over twenty-five years and an usher for ten, this was the first time I actually read an entire

Playbill. I finished and handed it to the husband, who then asked if I could describe the theater. With anxiety returning, I began with the standard speech about the size of the theater and the dates of construction when he put his hand on my arm to stop me, asking me to really describe what was going on. He reminded me that I was acting as the eyes for him and his wife. So I looked around, seemingly for the first time, and truly noticed the decor of the theater, the color of the curtains and the seats, the way the patrons were dressed, and imagined stories about what brought them all to the theater. I described the gaggle of kids that were leaning over the railing on the first level and peering down into the orchestra pit, watching the musicians in their own world as they practiced their music without regard to the audience or their fellow musicians. I noticed the demeanor of those on the sixth level who seemed excited to be in this grand theater for the afternoon compared with the casual demeanor of the patrons on the first floor, who seemed much more nonchalant about the impending show. I conveyed all of this to the blind couple until the patrons sitting next to them arrived, snapping me out of storytelling mode and prompting me to reluctantly vacate my seat.

I quickly rushed back to my post in the lobby only to find that I had been replaced! I was told to go back to the sixth floor with the blind couple and assist them for the rest of the show. I viewed this as a dismissal, but I didn't complain about the change (at least not outwardly, anyway), and went back to my new assignment on the sixth floor.

When intermission came, I went to the blind couple's location and asked if they were enjoying the show. They asked questions that I never answered before, such as what each of the actors looked like. What color and style were their costumes and how tall were the actors? I answered the questions to the best of my ability until again; I had to move when the patrons seated next to the blind couple returned. Knowing I would be subject to another round of questions at the conclusion of the show, I paid extra attention to the second half, trying to memorize every detail. That concentration paid off when I met the blind couple again and answered their questions as I escorted them back to the lobby to catch a cab home. The couple thanked me profusely for my assistance, stating that I allowed them to see so much more of the show than they would have been able to without my assistance.

Interestingly enough, I too was able to see so much more of the show because of their influence. Although I loved theater so much before, I love it even more after experiencing the show as the eyes of a blind couple. As a result of that moving and impactful experience, I now volunteer to do live audio description for the blind and visually impaired at several local theaters.

Lessons Learned: if you offer to help someone, do not be surprised or put out when they accept your help. Also know that helping people are a gift—and not only to those you are helping. Oftentimes, you get way more out of it than you actually give. Who knows—you may even find your calling!

> *"Everybody can be great...because everybody can serve. You don't have to have a college degree to serve. You don't have to make your subject and your verb agree to serve... You only need a heart full of grace. A soul generated by love."*
>
> -Dr. Martin Luther King, Jr.

Activation Steps

The first step in living an abundant life through service is to expand your definition of service. Service doesn't have to be through a non-profit organization, nor does it have to be helping someone in the traditional sense. It could be as simple as letting someone with less items get in line in front of you at the supermarket. Simply put yourself in the other person's shoes and think about how you would like to be treated.

Second, in seeking out opportunities to serve, think about that which is easy for you, but would mean so much to others. If you have lots of expendable cash but don't have much time, perhaps your opportunity is in making a donation. If you don't have cash, but you have time, perhaps you volunteer for a non-profit. If you don't have lots of time or cash, but you are healthy, perhaps you donate blood. If you see someone without a smile, give them one of yours.

If you want to go the traditional volunteer route, think of the things you love to do. In my case, I like education and theater, so I do both. If you like to travel, think about a volunteer vacation. If you like animals, think about volunteering for the zoo or the SPCA. Do you want a weekly, monthly or one-time commitment? Do you like exercising? If so, what about participating in a bike race, walk, or run to raise money for an organization? Do you love your work so much that you want to volunteer doing pro bono work in your field? This is something that lawyers often do but any professional from an accountant to a handyman or a Human Resources professional can make a difference by sharing their skills with a non-profit. Call your local United Way to ask about reputable organizations that meet

Kiss of Life

your specific interest. I assert that if you have an interest, there is an opportunity to volunteer doing it.

Finally, just do it. Like I said in one of my lessons, it's not about you; it's about others. So if it's fear that's stopping you, walk through it. If it's time that's stopping you, find something that doesn't take time. If it's money that's stopping you, do something that doesn't take money. If it's not knowing that's stopping you, ask others or look online.

Once you have that service experience, take a moment to be introspective and evaluate what you learned from the interaction. Maybe you learned, "I want to do something different next time." Or perhaps you learned that you have a newly discovered talent, or that making a difference in the life of another is a source of joy for you. Whatever the lesson, look for it, listen to it, take it to heart, and learn it well.

Sabrina Martinez

Spiritual Electricity
Good Things Come to Those Who Pray

On October 27, 2001, I became a single parent. It is not the day I gave birth or the day that my daughter's father left us, but the day my beloved mother lost her battle with colon cancer. It is a day that changed my life forever. It is the day I started to really depend on prayer.

My mother and I were very close. We had a bond that was unbreakable. I would not understand why we were so close until I had my own child. But we weren't always that close, or so I thought, because I felt that she was doing "more" for my brother than she was doing for me. It would be a long time before I was brave enough to confront my mother and when I did, I told her that she acted like she liked my brother better than she liked me. I stood the chance of getting a spanking that day, but it was a chance that I was willing to take. My mother's response to my accusations would stick with me forever and bring my confidence and self-esteem levels to an ultimate high. Mother told me that I was very smart, bright, and that I caught on very fast. I asked her how she knew that, and she said my teacher had called and told her. Then she said the best thing ever: she told me I was just like her. It's not that my brother wasn't smart, but he just liked to play around a lot, so my mother had to stay on him. She explained that she knew I could get my school work done on my own because I was so smart and cute, and she was right.

Spiritual Electricity

All of my life since I can remember, I have gone to church. In the beginning, I went with my grandmother because my mother worked on Sundays. I remember coming home and "playing church" with my cousin—she and I would pray and baptize each other and our baby dolls with a soda bottle filled with water. I would be the preacher and she would be the church lady. Every night before going to bed, I remember my grandmother getting on her knees and praying, and my cousin and I did the same. It is funny how you tend to recall your childhood or go back to your childlike ways when trauma strikes your life.

I have been to very few funerals in my life and I have had to "put together" only one in my lifetime, and that was my mother's. I remember being at the home that my mother and I shared, wondering who was going to do this heartbreaking task of arranging this funeral. I called my brother, other family members, and even friends of my mom's to no avail, either because they did not know what to do or they were just too hurt to help out. After calling several people for what seemed like a lifetime with no help in sight, I started bawling and just stood up in the middle of the living room and started praying out loud to God. I was pouring my heart out and asking Him to send me the help that I needed. Immediately after I said "amen," the phone rang and it was my mother's cousin who had been taking her to her chemo treatments and doctor appointments, and simply sat with her during the day while I was in college. He was calling to offer to help with the funeral arrangements.

When my mother passed away, I had many family members and friends call me to check on me and tell me to call them if I needed anything. The friends were people I have known for many years or friends of my mom's who had known her twice as long as I've known my friends. After about two weeks or so, most of the calls stopped. I know life goes on, but it was hard for me. I was in my last semester of school with a toddler and I didn't know how I was going to make it. Thank goodness I did have friends who stuck by me, including my college classmates and professors, but the problem was that I wasn't used to asking anyone for help other than my mother.

I decided that I would drop out of college to get a job so that we could stay in our home. I had to pray that I could find someone to watch my baby while I went to work. I got down on my knees and start praying, and suddenly, the phone rang. I let the phone ring and ring and ring until finally I stopped praying so that I could get up and answer the phone. It was a classmate of mine who was calling to check on us. I told her that I decided to quit school for financial reasons and get a job so that I could keep a roof over our heads and food on the table. But my friend absolutely would not hear it. She pointed out that I had come too close to accomplishing a major goal to quit, almost at the end. She said she would be at my house to pick me up the next morning, and she was there.

While I was still talking with her on the phone, there was another call coming in, so I ended the first call to answer the other. It was my babysitter calling to ask what time I wanted her to come pick up my baby. I told her that I really could not afford to pay her, so I was just going to quit school to find a job. The sitter was not hearing or having it either and she agreed to watch my baby until I graduated from college and found a job, and she would not accept payment. All of these blessings were bestowed on me even before I finished praying.

At that time in my life, I had not learned to expect and accept my blessings. I say that because even though I was just given two major blessings, I was still determined to quit school to find a job. I did not set my alarm clock that night to wake me up so that I could get up and get ready for school the next day. Little did I know that I was in for a frightening awakening, to say the least. At 6:00 a.m., I heard my mother calling my name to wake us up. It was loud and it was as if she were still in the house with the baby and me. Mom used to call my name every day to wake me up for classes and if I didn't get up quickly enough, she would send my baby in my room to hit me until I woke up. I tried to lie back down and go to sleep, but I could not on this particular day. The next thing I knew when I opened my eyes was that my baby was standing on the side of the bed with a big smile on her face, as if she were telling me to wake up like she used to when my mom sent her in my room to wake me up. I eventually got up and got dressed, and then there was a knock at the door. It was my second blessing that had been given to me the night before. This was the day I started to respect the power of prayer.

Being a single mom has been the most rewarding, joyful, dynamic, and oftentimes magical experience in my life, but it can also be pretty scary at times. This includes times when you have to make decisions for your children that can be life-changing and life-altering. There have been and still are times when I have had no one to talk to or go to and I have had to get on my knees or stop right in my tracks and just start to pray.

There will come a time in your life that you, too, will need help, and it will seem as if there is nothing or anyone you can call on for help. People will be busy, at work, and not able to take your call, or maybe even going through something themselves. It happens to all of us at some point and time in life. What will you do in that situation?

Your spouse or partner may not be available. Your mother or father may not be available. Siblings, family members, friends, and even children that you are used to depending on can't be found. Again, I ask, what are you going to do? Who will you run to? I encourage you to reach deep down inside your heart or go to that special place and call upon that higher power. I encourage you to walk by faith and not by sight. That's what I choose to do. I pray that you choose to do the same. I will always choose to activate my prayer power. I still depend on people, but only after I have prayed about my situation or circumstance so that God sends that special person or people my way. He may send someone you know, a complete stranger, or your beautiful child, filled with words of encouragement, a conviction, or verbal confirmation from God, as was often the case for me.

You too can activate the power of prayer and walk by faith, not by sight. If it has been a while since you have prayed or even if you have never prayed before, it can be done. All you have to do is get started.

Activation Steps

- ***Pray before you go to bed.*** Pray at night and in the morning before you start your day. If at all possible, include your family in praying with you; make it a daily and nightly part of your life.

Spiritual Electricity

- ***Develop a routine.*** If you would prefer to pray alone and do it in privacy, that's great, too. I often pray with my family and then after everyone is asleep, I go into more prayer about things that perhaps I don't want anyone else to know I am concerned about. If you have no privacy in your home, you can always pray in the bathroom or while taking a shower. Prayer does not have to be a long, drawn-out process unless you have several things to pray about. You can pray on your way to work or school and the best thing about prayer is that you can pray anywhere, any place, and anytime.

- ***Pray consistently.*** I don't necessarily mean pray about the same thing over and over again—that's your choice—but pray often, and pray about everything.

Let me tell you, I have not always received an immediate response or blessing each and every time that I prayed. Sometimes, your blessing may come with a delayed response, and other times a blessing won't come at all. In this situation, I have come to realize two things: either the timing isn't right for the blessing or God has something better planned for me. This is likely the case for you, too. I would suggest two things in this case. Sometimes I continue praying and other times I back off—whichever I am called to do, and you will also know what you are called to do because you will feel it deep down inside you. Whatever you do, do not totally stop praying.

The power of prayer has been a constant in my life since becoming a single mother. It has given me answers to questions that nobody else could answer and has helped me through some of my darkest and most traumatic times in my life. Now, when family and friends need prayer, they come to me. I am one of the go-to girls for prayer amongst my close circle of friends. I depend on answers from God for myself and others. But the newest and most rewarding part of prayer is that my now teenage baby now knows the importance of prayer. If a teenager can pray, so can you. It's not too late to start. Activate the power of prayer today!

Cheryl Smith

Smoke and Mirrors
Keeping Your Vision Crystal Clear

Have you ever found yourself in a situation that was unlike anything you have ever faced in your life? Imagine waking up one day feeling as if you were chained down, and the harder you pulled to be released from the chains, the more they seemed to tighten. The feeling leaves you bound, confused, frustrated, defeated, speechless, and afraid to take the next step. Then you begin to fall into a deep depression. As you fall into this depression, you begin to replay the different events in your head that have occurred in your life that led up to this very moment. Depression has become a daily struggle for you, because you have chosen to run from your reality. You begin to think, *will I live or die? Will I defeat this or not? Will I hinder myself from walking into my destiny?* Let's find out.

This is the way I felt a few years ago. While in the midst of this depression, I began to think back on the things that happened in my life that led up to this point. The first stop in my mind was to revisit my childhood as far back as I could remember. When I was seven or eight years old, my family moved from living in the house with my grandmother into the low-income community. We were so happy to move into a place we could call our own, but I missed living with my grandmother. I remember watching the women in our new community; some wanted more out of life and some wanted to do just enough to get their bills paid, nails done, hair done and material items needed for their children.

Being raised in a low-income community had its good days and its bad days, like most neighborhoods. In this community, there were very few fathers in the home taking care of their children and some of the women did whatever they could to make quick cash. Many of the women in the low-income neighborhood came in as babies and soon raised babies themselves.

My mother was one of those babies raising babies. As a child, you will discover that your surroundings can either help you make better decisions or direct you to make the wrong decisions. If someone had only told me that I was beautiful and worth the wait, I would have made some better decisions. These are the exact words I heard in my head as I laid down in the bed and gave away my virginity to a young man that did not deserve a gift so precious. But no one took the time to tell me I was worth more than a quick nut; I was worth waiting until marriage. I eventually fell for the same lines that some young men, who only had the idea of having sex, spoke to a young woman with virtue, beauty, and a prized possession—her virginity. I wished my father had been there to explain to me what love really looked like. But I would never know until it was too late to get it back. I was only fourteen years old at the time.

One of the smartest things I remember doing was giving him a condom to protect myself. As I watched him place the condom on, I also took a look at his face to see his expression. He showed excitement, but it was not the expression I was looking for him to have. I remember him lying on top of me and all I could think about was, *"Can you please get off of me?"* When he left, I felt so unclean that all I wanted to do was take a shower and clean myself. I also wondered why nobody told me I would feel this way. Instead, they spoke as though sex is the most amazing thing that has happened to them. For years, I have been looking for my father to tell me I am beautiful, but he has been so focused on finding love himself, he had no time to tell me. In order to make myself feel better about the situation, I convinced myself I was not running around like the other girls with every boy I met. I told myself that I was not being talked about like the other girls. But who was I fooling? I had given up my virginity and it was too late to say I am a virgin again.

As I went on to high school, I became well known for my character. I was very outgoing and fun to hang around with and my maturity level had reached an all-time high. I began to have business ideas like doing hair, so I created my first business in high school in the 10th grade. I had a clientele of about twenty people a week, paying anywhere from $30 to $100. That was a nice income for a teenager doing what I loved. I took a lot of the pressure off my mother by doing hair on my front porch. The money I made went toward my school clothes, school supplies, and miscellaneous things needed around the house. My home business did so well I was able to fix things on my car like the water pump, timing belt and get tune-ups when needed. My teenage years brought great joy, but I also had my share of pain at this time. I found this to be the most trying time in my life. As I began to actually date, I was tested by someone close to me.

My patience was tested, my strength was tested, my love was tested, and I was put in a position that no teenager should ever have to be placed in. I resented this friend in my life. As I was dating, I had no idea this friend had her eyes on the same man I had my eyes on. At the time, I had not slept with any of the guys I was dating because I was looking for someone with stability. At their young ages, the young men I dated at that time were not capable of giving me that. I was very mature for my age, at least that was how I felt. What I mean by mature is that I understood what I wanted out of life, and if someone did not have goals or some type of income to fit my standards, our relationship did not last long, and of course we did not keep the title of boyfriend/girlfriend for long. By this time, I was working in a hair salon after receiving my license as a hair braider. I also worked a second job and was living what I thought was *the life*. I learned a strong work ethic from doing hair on my front porch. I also treated my clients with much respect and the word of mouth promotion was amazing, because there was never a week that went by when I did not have spending money in my pocket and a bank account with money saved.

As I viewed every situation in my life from the minor events that occurred in my childhood to the events that took place in my teenage years, I noticed that I was holding on to the hurt I experienced from different events in my life. By holding on to the hurt and replaying the negative thoughts in my head, it began to lead me into depression. I noticed one thing I was still carrying around was the baggage of my past, and with that, I could not go any further. So I took a moment to think about the depression I was facing. I knew it would either take my life or I would have to make things right by getting to the root of the problem. I started working on the problem by first writing out all of the things I could remember that left a scar on me. I then began to write out apology letters, forgiving people who had hurt me, and releasing the individuals one by one. As I forgave each one, my problems seemed lighter. The weights I felt from this depression began to lift from my life. Despite how bitter I was on the inside, faith, love, forgiveness, and time alone in meditation helped me overcome my depression.

Smoke and Mirrors

At this point, I had faced low self-esteem, lack, doubt, fear, betrayal, and many other things. And the moment I looked back over my life and noticed that I continued to walk with my head held high, I forgave myself, I forgave others, I came out of a place of lacking, and I still went on with faith knowing that life had so much more to offer me than what I had experienced earlier in life. In that moment, I noticed I had been enduring a time of longsuffering. It was not meant to kill me prematurely, but teach me how to endure the blows that were thrown at me throughout this journey called life. And because of my faith, I lived through things in my life that would have pushed many others to the limit and caused them to take their own lives, give up, turn to drugs, steal, kill, or even turn to prostitution. It was actually crystal clear to me at that very moment. I had purpose deep within me. And no matter what I felt, I could not give up without pursuing my purpose. I could not die prematurely because there are others who are waiting to hear my story. And just like there are others waiting to hear my story, there are also people waiting to hear your story.

Once you let go of the fear and doubt, the little girl that wants to commit suicide will not commit suicide because of your story, and will push forward. The young man that wanted to go out and steal will stop in his footsteps, because he will think of a business idea that will allow him to make money so he does not have to steal from someone else, and end up in jail or dead. The teenage daughter will wait to have sex because she will acknowledge her worth and wait until marriage to give up her womanhood. The adult woman will look back over her life and notice mistakes, but will not allow them to hold her down. She will get up and move forward, knowing that her faith has brought her through her hardships. The fatherless will begin to forgive, not allowing the thoughts of the past to hold him or her back from the future that is ahead, allowing his or her father to start fresh and create a meaningful relationship.

As I began to release my past by surrendering to my future and acknowledging the woman I was becoming, I noticed a few things. This little girl image of myself was still appearing in my head, causing me to think as if I was this teenager again. When I had grown into a mature woman who made better decisions, I took the time to think about the decisions I made and how they would help or affect my future. With every step I took to get out of the depression, I saw another part of the teenaged me drop off, allowing myself to really live a life of abundance, freedom, and joy.

Activation Steps for Clarity

1. **Analyze your life.** Take the necessary steps to reanalyze your life and determine which areas you are lacking in and why. Then, you will receive a clear vision.

2. **Do the Work.** Start working on the problem by first writing out all of the things you can remember that left an impact on you.

3. **Surrender it all.** Apologize, forgive, and release individuals who have hurt you in some form or fashion. When you do, your problems will become lighter.

4. **Meditate!** It will help you to become clear and is an effective tool to help you stay focused.

The steps viewed will give you clarity on decisions you need to make and how to make them. For a person who receives a revelation about her life, it is like the light that reflects through crystal, causing the crystal to shine. Once you receive a revelation, it brightens your understanding of things you were unaware of until finding the cause of your situation. At that very moment, you will awaken and everything that was out of order in your life will come into alignment, and everything that made no sense will "click" and begin to make perfect sense.

Krystal Koi Jordan

Contributors

Nancy Matthews

Nancy Matthews is a speaker, author, and business advisor who combined her 25 years of business savvy with creative ingenuity and an intuitive understanding of people to bring about stellar results.

Author of *Visionaries with Guts*, *The One Philosophy*, and the highly acclaimed *Receiving Your Riches* course, Nancy has been featured on NBC, BraveHeart WomenTV, and the John Tesh Radio Network, and has shared the stage with some of today's leading experts such as Jack Canfield, Loral Langemeier, Kevin Harrington, and Bob Burg. Nancy is currently the CEO and Founder of Visions In Action, Inc. (her coaching and consulting firm), and Women's Prosperity Network (WPN). See more of Nancy and Women's Prosperity Network at www.nancymatthews.com or www.wpnglobal.com

Sabrina Martinez

According to Einstein, the meaning of life is "service to others." International speaker and author Sabrina Martinez lives by those words. A passionate volunteer, she spends countless hours making a difference using her experience in human resources and communications to serve as a community leader in education, the arts, and services for the blind. Whether volunteering or speaking to a crowd, Sabrina credits service as the secret to her success. See more of Sabrina at www.sabrinamartinez.com

Cheryl Smith

Cheryl Vanessa Smith is a mom, serial entrepreneur, dynamic speaker, blogger, author, career transitional expert, and well sought after vision board facilitator. She is the founder of MillionHeir Mom-*Dream It, Believe It, Live It*. She assists women, especially moms, with identifying their purpose, define their passion, and build a business so that they can spend more time with their families, especially their children. Cheryl's accomplishments include paying her own way through college, and being mom to a teenager who she hasn't strung up by her toes! She is also a co-author of the book "The GlamourLESS Side to Entrepreneurship: What They Didn't Tell You About Being A Women In Business!"

Cheryl's goals are to build a multi-million dollar international company, to start a foundation for women to start and/or complete their educational degree and to become a California-New York Snowbird! See more of Cheryl at www.cherylmillionheirmomsmith.com

Krystal Koi Jordan

Krystal Jordan is an entrepreneur, a mentor, a writer, a powerhouse speaker, and the mother of three amazing children. When you make God, family, and faith apart of everything you do, everything else will fall in place.

Krystal is a part of many organizations in her community, such as Klassy Kreations of God Inc.(Founded By Krystal Jordan),The Friends of the Library Tyrone Bryant Branch, The Young Professionals of The Urban League of Broward County, and Girl Scouts "Get Real" Mentoring program just to name a few. See more of Krystal at www.facebook.com/krystalkjordan

www.theartofactivation.com